Cambridge Elements

Elements in Economic History

edited by

Guido Alfani
Bocconi University

Latika Chaudhary
Naval Postgraduate School

Tracy K. Dennison
California Institute of Technology

Ewout Frankema
Wageningen University

Leandro Prados de la Escosura
Universidad Carlos III

John Joseph Wallis
University of Maryland

ORIGINS OF COLONIALISM

Why Geography Mattered

Tirthankar Roy
London School of Economics and Political Science

Shaftesbury Road, Cambridge CB2 8EA, United Kingdom

One Liberty Plaza, 20th Floor, New York, NY 10006, USA

477 Williamstown Road, Port Melbourne, VIC 3207, Australia

314–321, 3rd Floor, Plot 3, Splendor Forum, Jasola District Centre,
New Delhi – 110025, India

103 Penang Road, #05–06/07, Visioncrest Commercial, Singapore 238467

Cambridge University Press is part of Cambridge University Press & Assessment,
a department of the University of Cambridge.

We share the University's mission to contribute to society through the pursuit of
education, learning and research at the highest international levels of excellence.

www.cambridge.org
Information on this title: www.cambridge.org/9781009524179

DOI: 10.1017/9781009524186

When citing this work, please include a reference to the DOI 10.1017/9781009524186

First published 2025

A catalogue record for this publication is available from the British Library

ISBN 978-1-009-52417-9 Hardback
ISBN 978-1-009-52419-3 Paperback
ISSN 2977-1358 (online)
ISSN 2977-134X (print)

Origins of Colonialism

Why Geography Mattered

Elements in Economic History

DOI: 10.1017/9781009524186
First published online: March 2025

Tirthankar Roy
London School of Economics and Political Science

Author for correspondence: Tirthankar Roy, t.roy@lse.ac.uk

Abstract: Historians explain the eighteenth-century origin of European colonialism in Asia either with the profile of the merchants or an argument about uneven power. This Element suggests that the environment was an important factor, too. With India (1600–1800) as the primary example, it says that the tropical monsoon climatic condition, extreme seasonality, and low land yield made the land-tax-based empires weak from within. The seaboard supplied a more benign environment. Sometime in the eighteenth century, a transformation began as the seaside traded more, generated complementary services, and encouraged the in-migration of capital and skills to supply these services. The birth of a new state from this base depended, however, on building connections inland, which was still a dangerous and uncertain enterprise. European merchants were an enabling force in doing this. But we cannot understand the process without close attention to geography.

This Element also has a video abstract:
www.cambridge.org/origins-of-colonialism

Keywords: colonialism, British Empire, India, East India Company, Asian history

ISBNs: 9781009524179 (HB), 9781009524193 (PB), 9781009524186 (OC)
ISSNs: 2977-1358 (online), 2977-134X (print)

Contents

Preface

Historians explain the eighteenth-century origin of European colonialism in Asia either with the profile of the merchants or an argument about uneven power. This Element suggests that the environment was an important factor, too, and that place mattered. With India (1600–1800) as the primary example, it says that the tropical monsoon climatic condition made most inland states vulnerable. The seaboard had a more benign environment. Sometime in the eighteenth century, a transformation began as the seaside traded more, and some seaboard sites drew in capital and skills from the inland. What was special about these places? The answer is not the ethnicity of the actors but their geographical positions. Sections 1–4 build the narrative with the Indian case. Section 5 shows that geography is necessary to complete the story of origin in other cases, too, not in the same way everywhere.

I presented the topic before audiences with historians more knowledgeable of the scholarship than I was. The occasions included a seminar in the University of Geneva (2023), an international conference on 'Circuits of Exchange and Indian Ocean Hinterlands, c.1400–1800', jointly organized by the European University Institute and the Indian Institute of Technology Madras (2024); a seminar co-hosted by the Delhi School of Economics and the Indian Statistical Institute Delhi (2024); and a lecture at the Socio-Economic History Association, Japan, annual conference (2024). I am grateful to the participants for their comments and questions. My biggest thanks go to the Series Editor handling the project (Latika Chaudhary) and two anonymous reviewers who gave me three extremely useful reports while endorsing the project.

Most place names in the Element have changed, but the Element uses the old names to be consistent with the sources. An appendix table shows the modern names against the old names.

1 Introduction

Why Did Seaborne Trade Lead to Global Empires?

European intercontinental trade from the seventeenth century was a catalyst in the emergence of modern empires and in shaping world politics. Why did seaborne trade lead to global empires in Asia and Africa? Most answers to this question that are now available build around the profile of the merchants, their propensity and opportunity to play politics, or the capacity of the indigenous states to withstand or resist these moves. This Element will take a different line and suggest that environmental factors also shaped state capacity and state formation.

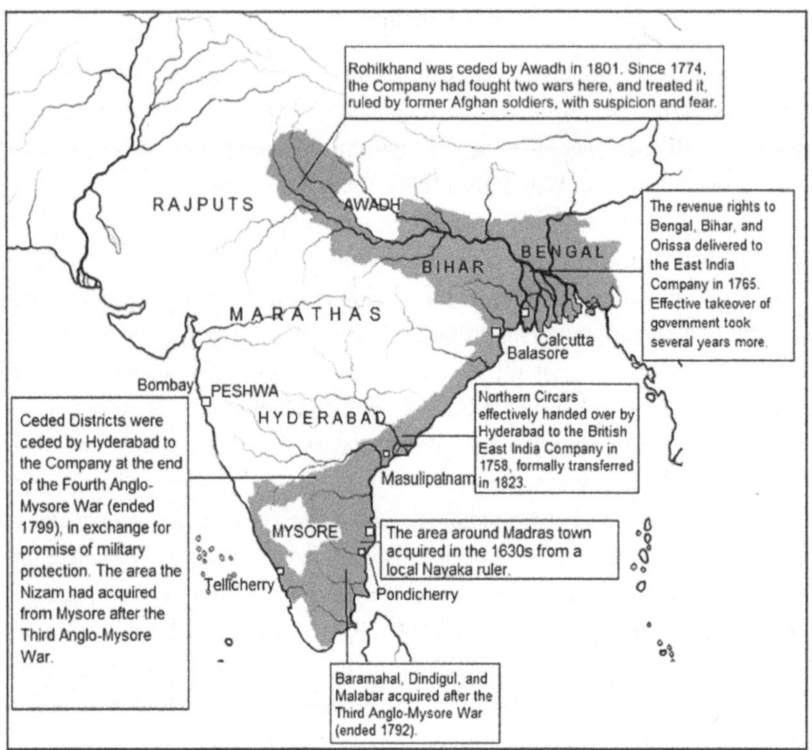

Map 1 India 1801 (British East India Company territories shaded).

Source: Author, based on data in the public domain.

That the Europeans came from a different political culture, commanded superior sea power, and in some areas were engaged in slave trades might tell us that empires were a result of some deeply embedded colonial ambition, military-political capacity, or coercive capacity. Such claims, common in many popular histories, are unverifiable, misread the purpose of intercontinental trade, and underestimate its risks and costs. These things matter, but we do not know if they do as the deep roots of empire.

In other versions, they had the backing of mercantilist states. Between 1688 and 1941, 'the English state constructed the fiscal institutions required to fund what became and remained the largest and most powerful navy in the world', effectively reducing the protection costs for British merchants overseas.[1] The British East India Company in Asia gained an advantage from the partnership between private capital and the state that supported England's 'fiscal exceptionalism', and the

---

[1] Patrick O'Brien, 'State Formation and Economic Growth: The Case of Britain, 1688–1846', in J. Backhaus, ed., *Navies and State Formation: The Schumpeter Hypothesis Revisited and Reflected*, Berlin: LIT Verlag, 2012, 217–272. Cited text on p. 226.

Dutch derived indirect benefits from it. As a theory of imperialism, the accent on power presumes that power mattered over negotiations and alliances. This is debatable.

Neither the idea of 'protection' nor the emphasis on firepower is new, though their use in early modern history has varied. In 1950, Frederic Lane 'emphasized ... in early colonial enterprise ... only one characteristic of government, supplying protection'.[2] In 2015, Philip Hoffman explained the connection between states and the capacity for organized violence with a model building upon the political fragmentation of early modern Europe. O'Brien's stress was on fiscalism. Stressing power differently, Philip Stern has shown that the British East India Company claimed the right to govern territories and British subjects overseas almost from its start. The company's founding principles permitted it to do that.[3] Stern suggests that these features should help us explain the origin of an empire in India.

These explanations concentrate on European agency and underplay how commerce and politics were changing in the places where the empires emerged. If, indeed, power mattered above all, we need to understand better the capacities of the states that were taken over. Before the eighteenth century, European power in India was negligible compared to the interior states that ruled inland, in areas well away from the seaboard. The Europeans in question were merchants and had little income besides returns on business investment. The interior states had large armies and a robust tax system to finance warfare. Why did the balance of power shift so radically?

The Company was a political type of firm, no doubt. But that fact would not account for colonization. It was also a business firm; like most business firms, risk aversion was a part of its character. Within the Company, there was a reverse pull towards commerce. The Company worked to earn money for its shareholders. Colonization was not a way to earn money; it was even wasteful, as some directors believed. With some exaggeration, we can claim that its capacity to enter negotiations with local magnates explains the emergence of many seaboard settlements that it started and how these were governed. It does not explain why some would survive and others die.

A second set of answers emerges from the historiography of early modern South Asia. The accent here is on conditions on the South Asian mainland, not in Britain.

---

[2] Frederic C. Lane, 'Oceanic Expansion: Force and Enterprise in the Creation of Oceanic Commerce', *Journal of Economic History*, 10 (Supplement), 1950, 19–31. Cited text on p. 31. Philip Hoffman, *Why Did Europe Conquer the World?* Princeton, NJ: Princeton University Press, 2015.

[3] Philip Stern, *The Company-State: Corporate Sovereignty and the Early Modern Foundations of the British Empire in India*, New York: Oxford University Press, 2011.

Theories of the Origin of a British Empire in India

In the nineteenth century, an imperialist reading explained the origin of the British Empire in India with anarchy left behind by the collapse of the Mughal Empire after 1707, with the death of Aurangzeb. The Company had to take up arms to save itself and save the collapsing state. This imperialist view was never accepted by empire scholars because it did not do justice to eighteenth-century history. Whether sympathetic to or critical of the British Empire, most historians acknowledged the presence of what C. A. Bayly called an 'indigenous component in European expansion'.[4] What was the most crucial indigenous component?

One answer points to the Mughal Empire: its structure, strengths, and weaknesses. In the seventeenth century, the great territorial power, the Mughal Empire, was strong on land but weak on the sea. The European merchant firms were strong on the sea but weak on land. These two blocks did not get along, but 'a balance of blackmail between land and sea' held both in check.[5] Illustrations come from Emperor Aurangzeb's quarrel with the British East India Company over protecting the hajj pilgrims against attacks by pirates (1686–90), which almost ended the Company's existence in India, and other episodes from the seventeenth and early eighteenth centuries. The land power feared the Europeans' naval might and the Europeans needed restraint in dealing with the former.

A crucial part of the picture is the Mughal command over sea power. The inland states in India, including the Mughal Empire, did not firmly control the seaboard. We should be careful how we interpret this fact. I will cite evidence later that compared with contemporary European states, the Asian empires lacked fiscal resources and that there was usually no cheap, easy, or safe way for the inland to access the seaboard or the opposite. It is also not certain that the Empire wanted to control the littoral. Fiscal capacity is only half right as an explanation for weak control of the sea.

The empire's priorities were different. The most powerful inland states collected land taxes from the fertile agricultural regions in the Indo-Gangetic Basin. In the Basin between market towns and beyond the northern borders with Persia and Central Asia, considerable overland trade existed, from which the states raised an income and procured horses for battle.[6] Like nearly all other tax types, trade taxes did not all reach the central treasury but were retained by local officers for their upkeep. Still, they provided a considerable income.

---

[4] Christopher Alan Bayly, *Rulers, Townsmen and Bazaars: North India Society in the Age of British Expansion 1770–1870*, Cambridge: Cambridge University Press, 1983, 5.

[5] Ashin Das Gupta, 'Indian Merchants and the Western Indian Ocean: The Early Seventeenth Century', *Modern Asian Studies*, 19(3), 1985, 481–499. Cited text on p. 494.

[6] Sumit Guha, 'Rethinking the Economy of Mughal India: Lateral Perspectives', *Journal of the Economic and Social History of the Orient*, 58(4), 2015, 532–575.

Aurangzeb's (1618–1707) expensive campaign in the Deccan at the end of the seventeenth century led to a loss of control over the regions, causing rebellions to break out, to which the rapid collapse of the empire after his death is sometimes attributed. When imperial power weakened, its access to local taxes also declined. The states succeeding the Empire did not necessarily gain. It appears that more of that revenue went to the local warlords rather than the successor states, which, too, lacked the political and military resources to create a strong form of federal power. As Asian empires weakened and, in the Indian case, collapsed, burdened by their troubles, the balance of blackmail ended, and sea-based power emerged as the kingmaker.

A variant of the thesis stresses merchants based in the few ports loosely controlled by these states. Dasgupta writes: '[T]he decline of the [Indian] maritime merchant [in the eighteenth century with the decline of West Asian and South Asian empires] contributed towards the foundations of the British empire in India.'[7] This explanation of the origin of British India – claiming that Mughal decline came first due to factors internal to it – starts from a premise the opposite of O'Brien's. The balance of power on land initially favoured the interior states. Only when the balance changed could maritime merchants play politics. '[F]rom the last quarter of the 17th century', the historian Sinnapah Arasaratnam wrote explaining the fall of Masulipatnam port, 'the Karnatak and Andhra lowlands saw unending political turmoil [,] one of the reasons for the decline of some of the vigorous ports of the earlier period'.[8] Ashin Das Gupta advanced a similar thesis for Surat, a major port on the western littoral. As politics shifted, Indigenous merchants suffered, the hypothesis goes.

The decline-first thesis is not persuasive. Apropos the decline of Indian merchants, it relies on observing a segment of coastal shipping that entered the European documents. A vast area of private commercial enterprise did not. The argument presupposes a dependence of commerce on politics. That premise works better for Surat and Masulipatnam, ports governed by big states (Mughal and Golconda), than Malabar or Bengal. In Malabar, the states were weak, scared of each other, and desperate to earn a share of trading profits. The most far-reaching interdependence developed between overland and overseas merchants, not between the state and the merchants. The Coromandel and Bengal situations were somewhere in between these two models.

More importantly, the decline-first thesis overlooks what happened in the eighteenth century. In the 1720s, Mughal power had started receding, yet a

---

[7] Ashin Dasgupta, 'The Maritime Merchant and Indian History', *South Asia: Journal of South Asian Studies*, 7(1), 1984, 27–33. Cited text on p. 27.

[8] Sinnapah Arasaratnam, 'Factors in the Rise, Growth and Decline of Coromandel Ports CIRCA 1650-1720', *South Asia: Journal of South Asian Studies*, 7(2), 1984, 19–30.

British Empire was still distant. In 1800, it was a reality. What happened in between? In the 1980s, a new theory of origin answered this question. What happened was not a conquest of the inland by a sea-based power. There never was a conquest of India. Instead, there were alliances. Bayly's work, admittedly confined to one small area in the eastern Gangetic Basin, claimed that the collapse of the Mughal Empire did not lead to anarchy but to the formation of regional states and consolidation of capitalism in the regions, a process that made alliance between Company officers and Indian merchants and states more likely.[9] In this group of indigenous allies, Bayly included members of a 'middle class', like the literate elites close to the regional courts.

If this reading emphasizes what some would call soft power, hard power matters, too. Military alliances were also prevalent and illustrate a similar dynamic. Conquest and warfare were not the appropriate terms to comprehend the Empire's emergence, as the British consistently had allies among Indians, and most of the rulers who allied with them ceded large territories in exchange for military assistance when required. The transfer of power in Bengal, the gift of Rohilkhand in 1801, and British power over Southeastern coast were results of alliances. 'Accommodations', as P. J. Marshall put it, were 'crucial to the rise of British ascendancy at every stage'.[10]

The alliance theory left two important questions unanswered, especially when dealing with military alliances. Why were the interior states so anxious to enter alliances? It would not be enough to say that the Company was the most powerful military force. It was not, despite a consequential victory in 1764 (Buxar). The British and French forces in mid-eighteenth-century India were formidable enough to be a sought-after ally. Still, militarily, they were not strong enough to prevail over most successor states, especially if some acted together. The Indians still had strong fortresses, powerful artillery trains, and thousands of horsemen. The commanders on the Indian side were not all competent strategists because command sometimes passed on in a family, but 'the numbers and resources they could bring into the field made them very formidable. The fighting was often of a most desperate nature. If there was any superiority of arms, it was not on the English side'.[11]

The European merchants with trading stations on the seaboard could command soldiers but had nowhere near the military capacity to win battles fought overland. Well into the eighteenth century, the British East India Company

---

[9] Bayly, *Rulers, Townsmen and Bazaars*, 5.

[10] P. J. Marshall, 'Presidential Address: Britain and the World in the Eighteenth Century: III, Britain and India', *Transactions of the Royal Historical Society*, 10, 2000, 1–16.

[11] Peter James Biddulph, *Stringer Lawrence: The Father of the Indian Army*, London: John Murray, 1901.

officers in India were obliged to match themselves with slow-moving infantry and a few field pieces drawn by oxen. The first standing armies consisted of runaway sailors, prisoners, odd Europeans seeking employment, and part-time Indian farmers. In Madras around the mid-eighteenth century, infantry soldiers came 'from factory doorkeepers and watchmen'.[12] The soldiers in Indian land armies, by contrast, were well-trained professionals.

Some states, like the Maratha factions and Mysore, learnt from the Battle of Buxar (1764) that consolidated British power in eastern India that they could get ahead of rivals by investing in a force that adopted some Western tools and ideas. This they did. The East India Company lost several times to Mysore and the Marathas and took a sound beating from the Rohillas in 1794 before the enemy mysteriously disintegrated. If all successor states could follow the example of the entrepreneurial warlords, why did they need the Company as a friend? Of course, the British Company had an incentive to offer their help if their proxy enemy, the French Company, offered their help to a rival party. But why did any Indian party need either the French or the British?

The missing piece in the puzzle is tax. The most militaristic successor states were in the relatively drier regions of India, with limited agricultural potential. Nearly all of them struggled to raise land taxes to consolidate their rule. A simpler way to get more tax was to acquire or bully weaker states; Mysore and Maratha warlords took that road. An unfinished struggle for finances made conflicts more likely, and conflicts made the struggle harder.[13] This geography-influenced chain – fiscalism-conflict-crisis – made alliances inevitable. The Company was just one of the parties with whom an alliance could be sought, though it might have been a more trusted ally given the nature of the organization and its outsider status.[14]

There is another unanswered question, the more crucial one for this Element. What factors accounted for the Company's ability to advance in the military contest in the long run? While not discounting the role of capital, technology, and organization, I want to stress geography – to bring the indigenous states' failure and the Company's success into a single explanatory model. The Company was not an interior state with weak fiscalism, weakening further with more conflicts. Its strength lay elsewhere. Its base in the seaboard offered it food security, an opportunity to forge connections with wealthy Indians, and

---

[12] George Fletcher MacMunn, *The Armies of India*, London: Adam and Charles Black, 1911, 4.

[13] I explore this dynamic in Tirthankar Roy, 'Rethinking the Origins of British India: State Formation and Military-fiscal Undertakings in an Eighteenth Century World Region', *Modern Asian Studies*, 47(4), 2013, 1125–1156.

[14] See Mandar Oak and Anand Swamy, 'Myopia or Strategic Behavior? Indian Regimes and the East India Company in Late Eighteenth Century India', *Explorations in Economic History*, 49(3), 2012, 352–366.

the ability to draw capital and skills into the spaces it controlled. For it, sustaining a military-political enterprise was, if not easier, not bound by the same challenges an interior state faced, starting with procuring food for an army. Even when the Company faced defeats, it bounced back quickly.

In the rest of the Element, I will build an alternative account of the origin of empire using the idea that *place matters*. The seaboard enters this account not as a source of naval might, as in O'Brien, but as a subsistence-secure and safe resource base. This accent is novel, and to show how it explains the origin of the British Empire, I should discuss more fully just how place matters. Geography comes in via two sets of distinctions: between an inland and a coastal economy and between an inland and a coastal polity.

Inland and Coastland

Stylized distinctions between land and sea are common in world history and often disputed. But I will give it a climatic spin that has not been used before. It works well for South Asia.

The 'land' is a tropical monsoon climatic space. Map 2 (and Map 3 in Section 5) shows areas with hyper-arid, semi-arid, or tropical monsoon climates. The common factor between all three zones is extreme heat during summer and seasonal rainfall. Parts of the tropics experience seasonal floods and rains owing to the actions of the intertropical convergence zone, known in India as the monsoon. The moisture influx is concentrated in a few months or even a few weeks in the year. The difference between the zones is in the strength of the influx: the hyper-arid receives very little water, the semi-arid about enough to sustain animal herding, perhaps one rain-fed crop, and the tropical monsoon has a longer agricultural year and better prospects of storing water for use in the dry season.

Extreme heat or aridity evaporates most surface water. In the past, when the monsoon was strong enough, it enabled agriculture, but aridity in the rest of the year kept the economically active season short. Outside these pockets, savanna ruled, where mobile animal herders lived. Variations in the volume and timing of rainfall, the only security against excessive heat, were extreme and unpredictable. Even minor variations in monsoon strength could cause natural disasters – floods, famines, and sometimes both together. Extreme seasonality of economic activity left most people busy for a few months and idle for a few months. The enforced unemployment constrained the incomes of individuals and states. Most artisanal work and trade occurred in the busy seasons, roughly three to four months after the end of the summer monsoon. If the monsoon failed, non-agricultural work collapsed, for peasants selling a new harvest could not buy anything. Disasters, thus, stressed incomes, savings, lives, and state capacity (see Section 2).

The seaboard in a tropical landscape is a distinct place, relatively resource-rich and famine-free compared with the drought-prone interior. In tropical monsoon Asia-Africa, that advantage would mean the ability to withstand climatic shocks, famine risks, and monsoon seasonality that restricted the business season to a few months in an agricultural landscape. Cyclones were more common on the seaboard, but not in all types of seaboard. In India, the Bay of Bengal experienced more violent storms than the Arabian Sea littoral. The seaboard was subject to seasonality but only in long-haul navigation. Whereas long-haul or intercontinental shipping was regulated by the monsoon, some short-haul or coast-to-coast shipping engaged in grain trade was shaped by the harvest cycle. Where the two things, monsoon and harvest, did not exactly overlap, the seaside trading town could, in theory, do trade all year round. Most places had the resources necessary (a deltaic situation, for example) for intensive agriculture or access to other livelihoods (like fishing and short-haul trade). The delta assured a year-round supply of surface water. In short, the seaboard was less susceptible to seasonality and disasters.[15]

There is a parallel set of contrasts between the coastal and inland polity. It is established that premodern states in Asia and Africa earned too little money per head to sustain a robust public goods drive.[16] Limited state capacity derived in South Asia from the poverty of the rural livelihoods that were taxed. In turn, the poverty derived from the extreme seasonality of agriculture, the main livelihood, thanks to its dependence on the monsoon rains. The tropical climate discouraged intensive cultivation almost everywhere and any cultivation over the vast savanna lands. Premodern states, and many modern ones, found it more challenging to tax herders than farmers. Frequent droughts limited the size and capability of states. The only way most states could deal with famines was to commute taxes, that is, by becoming weaker for the time being.

The Mughal army and bureaucracy did not save the empire from its critical dependence on a strong monsoon to survive. They were not rich enough to invest resources to control the seaboard or build a navy (see discussion above). Fiscally, they were weak and minimalist. During famines, the state retreated as taxpayers died. Peter Mundy, the merchant, observed heaps of bodies of people who had died of the 1630 famine lying for months outside the Surat city gates and wondered how

---

[15] See, for a fuller development of this argument, Tirthankar Roy, *Monsoon Economies: India's History in a Changing Climate*, Cambridge, MA: MIT Press, 2022.

[16] K. Kivanç Karaman and Sevket Pamuk, 'Ottoman State Finances in European Perspective, 1500– 1914', *Journal of Economic History*, 70, 2010, 593–629 (along with www.ata.boun.edu .tr/sevketpamuk/ JEH2010articledatabase) .

a state could fail so miserably to even clear dead bodies. The answer is simple: a drought left the state bereft of the capacity to perform basic duties.

Even if the state was fiscally weak to do other things, it could still command a military force effective enough to control a large territory. That advantage had less to do with fiscal prowess and more with the agreement among regional warlords to stay loyal to the central court and the economies of scale possible with the military enterprise. The core of the Mughal army was cavalry. The extensive use of the cavalry was not a natural choice in South Asia. It was a Turkic and Mongol legacy that persisted. It was an anomaly because the steed ordinarily used by these mobile armies was not indigenous to India and had to be imported. Extensive trading between Central, West and South Asia and horse markets on the borderlands sustained this mode of warfare. Any indigenous state that wished to match capability would need to spend enormous amounts of money to import horses. The cavalry controlled the Indo-Gangetic Basin, where lands were mostly flat and rich pastures occurred. A single horse-plus-rider was way more expensive to maintain than a single infantry soldier. And yet, because of the terrain, a rise in the size of the cavalry achieved a rise in cost advantage (the average cost of controlling one square mile fell) because the cavalry army could move quickly to cover a wider distance. A 30,000 square mile area could be controlled with an army meant to control 20,000 square miles and would not need a proportionate increase in size.

This scale advantage disappeared if the additional area had mixed ecological and geographical conditions. Hills and arid lands would require investment in a different sort of army than horses. The Mughal army had trouble in swampy Bengal and semi-arid Deccan. However, if the regions were loyal to the emperor, ruling the Indo-Gangetic Basin with this setup would not be a problem.

Similarly, a relatively rich state did not mean an equally robust military effort in all terrain if the scale advantage was missing. In much of the peninsular, this advantage did not exist. The Marathas relied on horses and gained a scale advantage, but the horses were different. The strategy did not work in conventional battles, and as their territorial power grew, an infantry army became necessary. The Malabar coastline illustrates the point especially well. If we project backward fiscal capacity data (tax per person or per unit of area) from 1900, then kingdoms that ruled in the present-day Kerala state in India around 1800 were richer than the neighbouring districts in Tamil Nadu. Even if cultivable land was limited, the semi-equatorial southwestern coast received a heavy monsoon and lesser degree of aridity than inland, food was cheap, droughts and famines were rare, and the states earned money from the stable output of tree crops like pepper. Its ecology was more benign than inland. Of course, much of this money did not reach a central treasury but was retained by warlords and landlords.

And yet, on this seaboard, a narrow strip of flat land, the appearance of high ranges near the coastline, and the heavy monsoon all militated against the cavalry army. Most armies on the western seaboard were infantry. With the agrarian hinterland too small, the infantry armies were small too and maintained by warlords and landlords. No kingdom here had a significant military advantage over the others. In the eighteenth century, an expanding military force inland, Mysore, exposed the entire western seaboard to instability.

Interpretations of the economic history of Southeast Asia characterize the early modern Indonesian archipelago as 'state-light', 'society-without-state', and a 'fragmented polity'.[17] Similar terms appear in descriptions of the tropical East African coast of the seventeenth and eighteenth centuries (see Section 5). It is not entirely accidental that European colonization happened in most of these areas of tropical and equatorial Asia and Africa. In almost all cases, the interpretations of limited state capacity point to the narrow tax base of the states because of their small agrarian hinterland and high-cost access to the interior or other islands.

The peninsular Indian seaboard represented a similar situation: fragmented state power, if not without states. European merchants did not automatically start to rule here. If they tried to, they would face the same problem, and in addition, would rival each other. However, a seaboard power that does establish secure connections inland would be ahead in the game because of the initial fragmentation. The British East India Company discovered that formula partly by the accidental circumstances of a thirty-year conflict with Mysore.

I will now combine some of these elements into a narrative of the radical shift in commerce and politics in the eighteenth century. The climate factor enters my story in a limited fashion to show that European commercial enterprise was robust enough, because of the strengths of the coastal economy, could plan ahead, and while the great seventeenth-century famines shook them up, these events also shaped a long-term diversification, a *spatial strategy*. I cannot say whether the inland polity suffered a disorder due to these famines or how big that was. There is not enough data to say anything about that with confidence. I make that claim, but it stays as a plausible inference in this Element.

In any case, the diversification moves led the British East India Company to the three areas where serious territorial acquisition began between 1760 and 1800 – Malabar, Bengal, and the Eastern Deltas (see Map 1). In two of these areas, getting trade licenses was easy because the local warlords and kings were

---

[17] See discussion in J. Thomas Lindblad, 'Changing Destinies in the Economy of Southeast Asia', in Tirthankar Roy and Giorgio Riello, eds., *Global Economic History*, Second Ed., London: Bloomsbury, 2024, 447–465.

eager to share in a profit of the trade. Negotiations did fail. But a small enough bribe could keep things in check. Approaching the Mughal provincial court for licenses was a much more complicated affair.

Politics was not the only distinction of these places. Wherever Europeans came to trade, trading began with a single commodity – pepper and textiles. However, the logic of commercial expansion drove the seaboard merchants to access a bigger basket of commodities from the inland economy – silk, sugar, indigo, timber, and saltpetre. That move drove the Company and private traders to build connections inland, often bypassing political orders. In Malabar and Bengal, that process had advanced much before colonization started. It had advanced in distinct ways.

In Bengal, knowledge of the interior meant knowledge of the river Ganges (Ganga in Map 2), the highway of overland trade in the Indo-Gangetic Basin. The English East India Company understood the river's significance and established factories along it – in Calcutta, Kasimbazar, and Patna. The local state also understood the river's significance, and their interest concentrated in Hooghly, Murshidabad, and Monghyr. Something similar happened in South India. Like the river, the crucial trade route was a well-defined one, passes through or gaps in the Western Ghats Mountain range. One pass, the Palghat Gap, was critical as a supply route and for military communication. As the Company realized in the 1760s to their detriment, the Mysore warlord had understood the significance of the mountain gap and built a secure fort there. The British, thanks to their contacts with merchants, could eventually wrest the pass from the Mysore warlords, and with that one move, secured the empire in South India.

As the eighteenth century drew to a close, the Company entered treaties and alliances with warlords and rulers all the time. Individual treaties broke down, but the propensity to form alliances was robust and survived. That enterprise, pursued for a long enough time, created a synergy of interests between merchants and bankers in the interior and those on the seaboard. It enabled the movement of soldiers and equipment between the two zones. In Bengal, the alliances, and in Malabar, that knowledge of the land was a crucial ingredient in the takeover of power.

Down south, the Company, with its infantry army, gained economies of scale with more secure control over the routes through which the army passed and a secure alliance with the traders and local kings who supplied grain to the army camps. It could now achieve something that an ambitious South Indian warlord could dream of: an overland link between the western and the eastern littoral. Madras on the east and Tellicherry on the west, with stations in the Baramahal area in the middle (see Map 1), became points on a single axis. This is why

Figure 1 Squall over Madras with Fort St. George in the distance, William Daniell, c. 1833. Although a resource-rich coastline, cyclones on the Coromandel evoked fascination and fear and was the subject of many paintings from the eighteenth century.

Source: Alamy, public domain image.

holding the Palghat Gap – simultaneously a road connecting the western with the eastern seaboard, a fertile rice growing area, and a settlement for grain merchants – could change the balance of power in South India.

The Eastern Delta, the Northern Circars, was a gift from Hyderabad and not commercially central. Some Company officers were aware of its future potentials. The region would lead a green revolution a century later. Fertile soil, plentiful water available from the large river deltas, export trade, flourishing manufactures, an absence of wars and raid, and 'the free secure enjoyment of private property' made this one of the more peaceful tracts in the second half of the eighteenth century.[18] The only problem, and this was a big one, was exposure to extremely intense cyclones that the Bay of Bengal was notorious for (Figure 1).

If the seventeenth century was marked by diversification of bases, the eighteenth century saw some of these bases build secure links with land. Throughout, indigenous merchants joined the enterprise where they could. They would do more in the nineteenth century. The third factor besides resource and trade connections, which I call the agglomeration effect, was the propensity

---

[18] Charles Greville, *British India Analyzed. The Provincial and Revenue Establishments of Tippoo Sultaun and of Mahomedan and British Conquerors in Hindoostan Stated and Considered*, London: R. Faulder, 1793, Part 1 of 3, 239.

of indigenous businesses to migrate to the towns and cities under European control. The second half of the eighteenth century in India saw such migration extensively.

The incoming wealth substantially improved taxability and credit markets in these towns, while the interior urban centres were drained of both. Trade generated complementary services, such as finance and marine insurance, and where the factor markets were open, it enabled more migration of capital and skills to supply these services. In the nineteenth century, two relatively new trades, indigo and opium, encouraged a wave of migration into the port cities, engaged in funding the production of these commodities, the auction houses, and as representatives of Manchester firms.

To summarize the stylized narrative, the coastland offers food and water security against a drought-prone inland. That disparity played a role in eighteenth-century Indian history, together with the commercial processes that created hubs on the coasts, to aid a divergence in political and economic power between the inland and the coastland. However, where in the coastland business efforts would concentrate did not depend on a plan. Accidents shaped that pattern. A string of coastal settlements emerged in the first stage. The long-term business prospects of any of these places depended not just on food and water security but also on access to inland goods. A subset of these places could build that access, usually by collaborating with inland merchants. In a second stage of the narrative, a reverse movement from decentralization to concentration occurred depending on where these access routes opened. If these routes were good for trading, they were also good for troop movement and extension of power, if need be. In the third stage of the process, settlements acquired the ability to become cities and attract private capital, who sustained power not as collaborators or business partners but as taxpayers, administrators (of cities), agents of globalization, and by firming the imperial economic system.

This stylized three-variable (security, connection, agglomeration) narrative helps us understand India through three centuries. Without any one of these elements, the origin of colonialism in that region cannot be properly explained. It does not explain colonization in most other parts of the world in the same way. It does not work well for regions where the coastland places were transit ports to start with, or points of the slave trade, or equatorial, or where the would-be imperial power needed to build different sorts of ties with the inland. However, the three ingredients – security, connections, and agglomeration – can still be found at work in Asian and African cities that started to grow rapidly in the late nineteenth century. I will show in Section 5 that the accent on resources, inland access, and agglomeration is useful in thinking about the origin process beyond India.

There is an argument implicit in this account that connects urbanism with empire. The intuition behind that link (and Section 4) is that empires, at least the British Empire, survived thanks to a compatible relationship between private capital and state power. Private investment may conjure up expatriate capitalists. In fact, the greatest fields of investment in nineteenth-century Asia and Africa – overland trade, coastal trade, and finance – engaged indigenous capitalists. Their business history is still a patchwork. There cannot be any doubt that indigenous merchants and bankers were the axes of the capitalism that formed under the British Empire and were critical to British power. Two episodes from Indian history illustrate the connection. During the greatest crisis of the empire in 1857, merchants and the port cities stayed loyal to the regime. The Rebellion of 1857 was a revolt of the inland, where the Company was an outsider, and the old warlords had suffered; the revolt failed because the coastlands steadfastly backed British rule. Even inland, merchants and bankers overtly or secretly helped the Company.[19] During a second crisis, post-Depression, indigenous capital started funding the nationalists and turned its back on the Empire, sealing its fate.

Contemporary writers of the British Empire understood this link perfectly. Nineteenth-century intellectuals who rationalized the Empire pointed at its role as an enabler of trade, making no distinction about the ethnic groups that were trading. A similar bias for the coastlands was present in imperial policy in Africa and Southeast Asia, too, a factor that saw Indian and Chinese businesses migrate using imperial contact points and routes.

In the previous section, I have carefully avoided talking about Bombay, Madras, and Calcutta – the three port towns the British East India Company had started in the seventeenth century – because their role was minor and uncertain during the first two phases of this narrative. The three towns represented different patterns of urbanism until late in the eighteenth century, when the concentration of defence capacity led to a convergence (Section 4). All were under various threats in the eighteenth century, even threats to their existence. It was only in the third stage, agglomeration, that these cities contributed to the state formation process.

Counterfactuals

In insisting that coastlands had natural advantages that need to figure in a story of the emergence of colonial rule that has so far been too political, I need to tackle two counterfactuals.

---

[19] Tirthankar Roy, 'The Mutiny and the Merchants', *Historical Journal*, 59(2), 2016, 393–416.

 Economic History

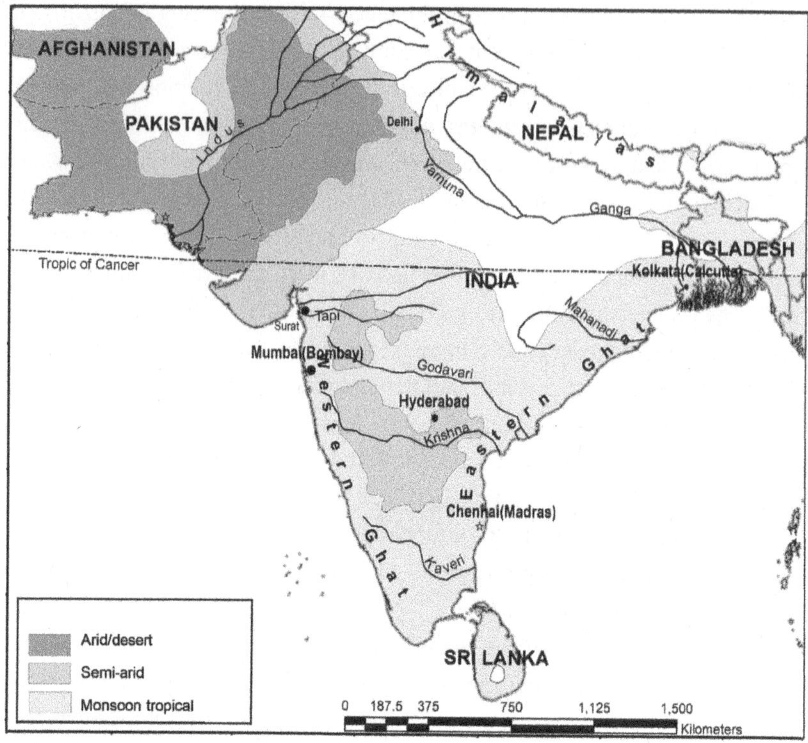

Map 2 India climate zone, present.

Source: Author, based on data in the public domain.

Surely, the Dutch or the French could do it too in India? The coastlands were a cosmopolitan trading zone for centuries. All merchants operating on the seaboard – Gujarati, Arab, Chinese, Dutch, French, and Danish – had equal access to a benign environment. What made the British special? The British enjoyed no more advantage than the Dutch, Portuguese, or French. It is futile to seek an explanation of their advantage in institutions, infrastructure, managerial ability, or Britain's fiscal exceptionalism. The only credible explanation is that the British East India Company was far more active in its spatial strategy than its competitors, whether Indian or European. It operated from many sites, nearly all of which failed to survive and grow. Eventually, a few bigger ones drained them of capital and skills. Yet that initial investment placed them in a strong position when conflicts broke out. At the very least, it gave them more ways of moving men and material.

Why did the British display this propensity? The word 'strategy' makes this process sound more deliberate than it was. A strategy there may have been. But the process was also shaped by experiments and accidents rather than planning.

The problem of private trade was critical to explaining the chaos and unpredictability of the diversification process. The monopoly charter handed by the British Crown to the Company leaked right from the moment it was first delivered. The Company had a trade monopoly thanks to the charter, but the monopoly was not enforceable outside Britain. Private traders disobeyed it and got away because local rulers had no incentive to respect the royal charter. Private traders, sometimes a handful of people, would reach an unknown shore area, negotiate with landlords who were generally very open to enter deals, and start trading. They had a propensity to choose places where the Company did not have a base. But if they were successful, the Company would try to create a base there to pre-empt their business.

More often, private traders established covert commercial alliances with Company personnel. Even though they knew this, the London directors could not prevent conflicts of interest beyond levying small fines. As a result, the division between the Indian branches and the central office grew. The former took most decisions about resettlement and opening new ports, and increasingly, in the eighteenth century, vital military-political ones as well.

On the Konkan coast, new settlements came up thanks to the formation of a rival East India Company by William Courteen.[20] The old Company followed him to ensure he did not gain an advantage. In the Godavari Delta, private traders were rampant because, in the absence of a powerful local state, they had as good a playing field as the Company. The Company had to follow them to ensure they did not gain an advantage. Officers of the Company secretly wanted to profit from private trade. In 1674, a young merchant Thomas Pitt reached the Company's settlement in Balasore and set up an independent trading concern in defiance of the Company's prohibition. Shrewdly, he married the daughter of a Company officer there. Unable to punish him, the Company made him the governor of Madras. This colourful figure later became famous for possessing one of the world's largest diamonds, which he had acquired from a merchant in Madras in 1702. Most smaller places in this way displayed the disorganized and bottom-up ways that diversification happened with the English Company. The Dutch and the French relied more on top-down diplomacy in selecting places. Where they settled, they were more powerful than the English (for example, Cochin, Nagasaki), and could bar them entry, but they settled in fewer places.

A second counterfactual is this. An inland state could just as easily spread out to the littoral. Why did that not happen? That story is unlikely for several reasons. My reason for thinking it unlikely for India is the weak fiscal capacity

---

[20] Neelambari Jagtap, 'Ports, Markets, Commercial Networks, and Politics: Case of Tal (South) Konkan in the 17th Century', in Radhika Seshan and Ryuto Shimada, eds., *Connecting the Indian Ocean World. Across Sea and Land*, London: Routledge, 2022, 83–92.

of the inland states, thanks to seasonality and low yield of land. We should not get carried away by the spectacular architecture and the enormous army of the Mughal Empire to think it was a strong state. It was not. The army formed of coalitions; if a significant number of the coalition partners broke away, the empire would collapse, as it eventually did. Its bureaucratic reach was confined to a small area within the Indo-Gangetic Basin, a fraction of the much larger area it earned tribute from and on which it collected little information. The universal reason why the inland agrarian zone could not easily expand is that the seaside situation mainly traded, and the inland zone mainly produced. These were different worlds. Trade generated complementary services, such as finance, and where the factor markets were open, it enabled more migration of capital and skills to supply these services. The inland world was less changeable because agricultural land was fixed in space.

I am exposed to a familiar criticism in drawing a sharp distinction between the seaboard and the inland. It is neither a new idea nor an uncomplicated one. S. Arasaratnam suggested something similar in a collection of his essays. Other historians, such as K. N. Chaudhuri and Sanjay Subrahmanyam, have felt the distinction was overdrawn.[21] I am not swayed by this debate. Arasaratnam offered a concept based on state formation. I base the distinction on climate and seasonality, something more solid and durable than politics. The counter-example comes from exceptional actors, a handful of ship-owning state elites who cannot have much agency in generating broad-based market integration.

No doubt considerable trade existed between the rural interior and the seaboard. Still, such trade depended on waterways that did not function throughout the year, roads that were difficult to access, and merchants who specialized in maritime or overland trades. Only in the Indo-Gangetic Basin, and there too seasonality was extreme, did the rivers have ports inland. Almost no river had much navigability in the peninsular, and long-distance traffic depended on the expensive and low-capacity bullock caravans. Along with state capacity, geography separated the two spheres until the railways of the nineteenth century truly bridged the gap and integrated commodity markets. Before that, 'bridging the gap' would require considerable diplomatic and political skills, as well as mercantile alliances. The Company managed to command that. The inland states did not.

The Element will not say that the European merchants could foresee these attributes and plan to use them decades, even centuries, after their first tentative

---

[21] See David Washbrook, Review of Sinnapah Arasaratnam and Aniruddha Ray, *Masulipatnam and Cambay: A History of Two Port Towns 1500–1800*, and S. Arasaratnam, *Maritime Trade, Society and European Influence in Southern Asia, 1600–1800*, in *Journal of the Economic and Social History of the Orient*, 39(4), 1996, 465–467.

settlements. Politics intruded on this process in entirely unpredictable ways. There were numerous false starts, settlements were started and abandoned, places were attacked, and people got caught up in conflict. There was a prominent role for accidents, luck, and unforeseen developments behind the transformation of a coastal village into a commercial-political-military hub. But these conditions were necessary and increasingly sufficient for hubs to acquire political-military power from the turn of the nineteenth century.

This Isn't about 'Port Cities'

Some historians reading this Element will try to connect it to a familiar literature on port cities. This scholarship has studied the seaboard towns through their common functions – mainly maritime trade.[22] This Element differs in its accent. My primary interest is not in maritime trade or how the maritime transformed places. Rather, it is the sustainability of any single site to attract capital and people and conduct trade.

'Ocean-adjacent port cities in the period between 1500 and 1800', writes Jessica Roney, '*did* share distinctive traits that allow us to consider them as a discrete category'.[23] Similarly, port cities have been studied through demographics and culture, such as exposure to disease, immigration, diversity, and common commercial culture, and through their role in sustaining regional circuits of exchange.[24] Port cities were similar in some ways. But that does not explain patterns of political shifts, which were more diverse.

The port city concept connects port cities and finds common elements (migrant merchants) and differences (distinct networks) between them. That approach leads to a circularity: port cities were those that served a port function. Michael Pearson's claim that 'Surat and Mombasa have more in common with each other than they do with inland cities' is valid but does not help us see the very different ways empires formed in South Asia and East Africa.[25] The littoral is not alike. Their geographies (resource cost, trade cost, agglomeration potential, climatic risk) were different. The difference mattered to politics.

The port city scholarship is relevant in a different way. It shows us that some places like Batavia were successful not because of benign climate (Batavia was notorious for disease) but for their transit functions. The transit port challenges the

---

[22] Frank Broeze, ed., *Brides of the Sea, Port Cities of Asia from the 16th–20th Centuries*, Kensington: New South Wales University Press, 1989.

[23] Jessica Roney, 'Introduction: Distinguishing Port Cities, 1500–1800', *Early American Studies* (special issue), 15(4), 2017, 649–659.

[24] Robert Lee, 'The Socio-economic and Demographic Characteristics of Port Cities: A Typology for Comparative Analysis?' *Urban History*, 25(2), 1998, 147–172.

[25] Michael Pearson, 'Littoral Society: The Concept and the Problems', *Journal of World History*, 17(4), 2006, 353–373. Cited text on p. 354.

Indianist framework I have outlined so far, one in which land figures more prominently than oceanic networks. Section 5 comments on the contrast and what it means.

This Element does not deliver a detailed account of how European merchant firms came to India and built their commercial interest. But a few bare facts are in order.

Indo-European Trade

In 1498, a Portuguese mariner, Vasco da Gama, reached Calicut, a seaport on the Malabar Coast. He was the first European mariner to complete the journey from Europe to India via the Cape of Good Hope. He demonstrated that Western European merchants could reach India without travelling overland in West Asia, a hostile route for several reasons. In a little over a century following this event, the Portuguese, English, and Dutch established trade links between Europe and Asia. In the late seventeenth century, other nations joined the contest for a share in the Indian Ocean trade (Figure 2). The records left by these traders revealed a world of commerce in the seaboard societies of southern Asia that was older and bigger than European trade in the Atlantic Ocean.

In the seventeenth and eighteenth centuries, European enterprise on the Indian seaboard was a link first in Asian trade and then between tropical products and Western Europe's emerging mass consumption habits. These merchants collaborated with many indigenous businesses, but we can only know a little of that world in detail based on European sources. Questions about their scale and long-term trajectory remain unanswered. There is no question that European trade brought many of these businesses into a networking relationship. Collaboration rather than competition was the more common characteristic of that relationship. On the other hand, Indo-European trade intensified competition between these foreign firms.

Between its establishment in 1600 and the unofficial takeover of Bengal in 1765, the joint-stock firm nicknamed East India Company (English before the union of 1707, British after) had amassed substantial riches and influence. It had helped to build a commercial infrastructure, including docks, warehouses, and overseas settlements, which was funded by the proceeds from international trade. Its entry into India in the 1620s occurred as licensed settlements in ports owned and managed by inland states. However, like its political rival, the Portuguese, and commercial rival the Dutch East India Company, it was constantly looking for convenient places where the difficult negotiations with territorial empires could be avoided. That drive led the Company's commercial activities to shift (relatively speaking) from western and southern India towards Bengal, Malabar, and the Eastern deltas in the eighteenth century.

Figure 2 Dutch Graves, Chinsurah (Chunchura) from seventeenth and eighteenth centuries.

Source: Author.

Like the English East India Company, merchants and shippers set up the contemporary Dutch East India Company with a monopoly charter to trade in the East. Unlike the former, the charter came from the Estates-General, the legislative body of the Dutch Republic, the government that controlled the Netherlands from the late sixteenth century until the French Revolution. The charter granted the Company sovereign powers, sanctioning the Company to turn into a quasi-state with its army, navy, and a largely hereditary bureaucracy. If that made for limited interference from politics in the commercial activities, the same problem of a divergence between the head office and the branches that plagued the British counterpart existed here, too. Between the two, accounts never tallied, and the branches were not closely coordinated.

Initially, the Company's business was in Indonesian spices. In the second half of the seventeenth century, it procured textiles from India partly to pay for spices and increasingly as an independent business. In the late eighteenth century, the most extensive commercial operations were in Surat, Bengal, and Coromandel, accounting for 80 per cent of the profits.[26] However, the textile

---

[26] Justus M. van der Kroef, 'The Decline and Fall of the Dutch East India Company', *The Historian*, 10(2), 1948, 118–134.

business was under pressure from British competition in Bengal. The Company's Southeast Asian operations were then making little money because the spice trade had shrunk, and thanks to monopoly control, little capital other than the Company's own came into these regions, leaving the Company inclined to collect tribute from local rulers. A significant difference between the British and the Dutch Company was the former's greater openness to in-migration of local merchants into the Company towns. The Company was liquidated in the wake of the French Revolution, and the territories under its control were passed over to the Dutch government.

The French move into India began in 1666 with the establishment of an East India Company. The French state issued a charter, and in the political context of the time and given the late entry, implicitly committed to more central support. Bases came up in Calicut, Surat, Masulipatnam, Mahe, Karaikal, Yanam, and others. Eventually, the bases at Pondicherry (1673) and Chandannagar (1688), the former becoming the headquarters of French India in 1701, took away a lot of the investment from the old ones.

The French East India Company struggled to make ends meet in the seventeenth century. Its scale was too small, and the competition was too fierce for it to command much credit in the Indian money market. Letters from Surat complained of dire conditions.[27] The arrival of Joseph François Dupleix in Chandannagar led to a revival. Dupleix used his contacts with Indian merchants in Bengal and Coromandel effectively to build a growing commercial enterprise between 1730 and 1754. He foresaw that succession disputes within fiscally weak states in southern India represented an opportunity to enhance French political authority and used that to drive the English out of India.

From the 1740s, French enterprise was caught up in Anglo-French rivalry too deeply to develop trade. The Treaty of Paris in 1763, also the year of Dupleix's death, temporarily ended the rivalry. Numerous efforts were made to restore French dominance in India between 1763 and the Napoleonic Wars, but none received significant backing with troops or money from the parent state. At the end of the Napoleonic wars, the British Indian customs ensured that much of the French trade in Pondicherry stayed confined to the local areas.

The Danish East India Company was established in 1618. The hub of Danish trade in Asia was Tranquebar, in present-day Tamil Nadu, but the Company also operated in Bengal and Malabar (and Macassar in Celebes in Indonesia). Unlike its European counterparts, the Company was engaged more deeply in intra-Asian trade, possibly taking a bigger part in the seventeenth-century slave

---

[27] Aniruddha Ray, 'The Crisis of the French East India Company at Surat and Bengal at the End of the 17th Century', *Proceedings of the Indian History Congress*, 54, 1993, 361.

trade in Asia. The Company never gained much of a foothold in India because of fierce competition from the Dutch and the English, which its weak organization and financial situation could not cope with. A disturbed relationship between the Company, on the one hand, and the Mughal Empire and some Indian merchant groups, on the other, did not help either. It wound up in 1729.[28] The Swedish East India Company was granted a royal charter in 1731. It traded in Asian articles, mainly procured in China and India, and sold Swedish iron and other goods there. The business was constrained by the Company's reluctance to acquire a secure base in India and, indirectly, underinvestment. In 1813, the Company liquidated.

The summary should explain why the narrative pays relatively more attention to the British and Dutch traders and trading firms.

A Restatement of the Thesis and a Plan

The central premise of the Element (which should help to draw lessons from India that can be applied elsewhere) is that in the tropical monsoon regions, the coastland had a significant intrinsic geographical advantage over the inland. That advantage stemmed not from maritime trade as such but from greater security of food and water. Indo-European trade saw that advantage being exploited more thoroughly for intercontinental commerce. There was no inevitable link between that fact and the emergence of a British Empire in India. Still, the British diversification moves and attempts to forge connections with indigenous capitalists in many places made an engagement with politics likely. Eventually, the partnership between capital and empire drained the interior of finance and skills. It led to a concentration of capital in the coastland, securing and strengthening the coastland as a seat of power. Places matter.

While historians of colonialism typically stress the pursuit of political opportunism or the combatting of political threats, the Element stresses geography. What mattered for any settlement to expand were three things: resource base – in tropical monsoon Asia-Africa, that would include the ability to withstand climatic shocks, famine risks, cyclones, and seasonality; trade and transport cost, especially access to the interior via safe routes; and the ability to attract local private capital and skills. Some, not all, seaboard settlements had – or acquired – all three qualities to help seaborne power become terrestrial. European trade was the agent that brought these elements together to form a powerful combination. Places with better 'provisions', which could also

---

[28] Kathryn Wellen, 'The Danish East India Company's War against the Mughal Empire, 1642–1698', *Journal of Early Modern History*, 19(4), 2015, 439–461.

access a diverse basket of goods, connect a diverse set of businesses and attract local capitalists, grew to shape political fortunes.

The three sections that form the narrative of the Element are organized chronologically. The next section, about the first chronological phase, concentrates on the seventeenth century. This was when indigenous states controlled port cities. Indo-European and European merchants had to align with a landscape that the indigenous states had created. This is well known. Less well understood is that the seventeenth century, and especially the second half of it, was also a time when there was a struggle to reduce that dependence and create zones where the European merchants controlled the infrastructure and trade routes overland and overseas. Politics motivated these movements. The climate did, too.

2 Escaping Famines in the Seventeenth Century

In one volume of the English Factory Records compilations, the words related to food and famine occur about thirty times. What does this suggest to us? Browsing the factory records, anyone can see that the great seventeenth-century famines occurring in 1630 and 1661 underscored two things. A seaboard location for trade was a relatively low risk one from a survival point. And not all seaboard places were suitable for escaping famines, for trade, and to build settlements. A new awareness of the environment and environmental risks would shape the perception and choice of places among the English merchants, devising an India plan there. Diversification from original bases to a cluster or interconnected network was needed.

As a general rule, the seaboard towns had, if not cheaper food, more variety of food. It was cheaper to import food over water than over land. Therefore, they could better withstand famines that struck the arid tropics like clockwork. Even in the harshest climates, the seaboard had a better chance to overcome heat and seasonality. Most seaside places could access the stable flows of a deltaic river, and sometimes by trading with the rest of the world, reduced their dependence on agriculture.

Successful ancient ports of India required a band of fertile cultivable land around them. This was the case in Surat. The historian of medieval Bengal Aniruddha Ray thought that the ports could barely pay for their governance from taxes collected from merchants and needed a tax base outside their boundary walls.[29] Tax rates on trade were generally low; an uncompetitive rate would drive merchants to another port. Trade income being almost impossible to know,

---

[29] Aniruddha Ray, 'Shorosh shatabdir sheshbhage Banglar nagarbinyas o arthanoitik samriddhi', [Urban and Economic Expansion in Bengal towards the End of the Sixteenth Century, in Bengali] in Gautam Chattopadhyay, ed., itihas Onusandhan [History Research], Calcutta: K.P. Bagchi 1986, 20–34.

taxes were charged on commodities. A high commodity tax would defeat the purpose. And finally, as S. Arasaratnam observed (see fn 52), most Indian ports were seasonal and earned money only for a few months in a year. For all these reasons, ports needed a little captive agricultural tract for additional income and to survive bad seasons.

Conditions were very different inland. Often, a few miles outside the city gates, conditions changed.

Satyasyo Kal

On 11 November 1630, Peter Mundy set off from Surat to go to Agra, probably on an assignment of the East India Company. Mundy (1596–1667), known as the son of the merchant Richard Mundy of Cornwall, is otherwise an enigmatic figure among merchants who kept a diary. These writings were largely unknown in Mundy's lifetime. He left detailed accounts of travels in Europe, West Asia, Western India, China, and Japan, covering more than fifty years, most of which remained overlooked, if not unknown, until 1902.

As soon as the party stepped out of the boundary of Surat town, they saw on the roadsides bodies of people who had died from a great famine. Large groups of people joined the highway in search of someplace where there was food. Mundy's party were under constant threat of attacks by half-starved wanderers. They could get scarcely any food and little fodder. On 30 November, they reached Burhanpur, where conditions were somewhat better. Mundy heard in this town, which had good communication with northern and western India, that the famine had begun with the failure of the monsoon rains in Gujarat that year. The exact sequence of events that led to the devastating 'satyasyo kal' or the famine of '87 (1687, by Vikram Samvat calendar) is unknown. Famine conditions raged over three years, as one monsoon failed and the next flooded the croplands. Two years later, the ruin was even more dreadful when he returned to Surat by the same route. Town after town had been deserted. Diseases had carried off many people. Back in Surat, several employees at the East India Company factory were dead. Mundy speculated, on what basis we do not know, that a million people had died in Western India from the famine.

Meanwhile, Surat's officers (factors) registered their accounts of the famine. Although some officers died in 1631–32, it is unlikely that they died from starvation. More likely, they fell victim to diseases. The factory records talk about the famine as if mass deaths affected others, not them: 'God's heavy wrath' descended upon 'these people'.[30] But business was very bad. Textiles

---

[30] Citations in this paragraph and the next two are from William Foster, *The English Factories in India 1630–33*, Oxford: Clarendon Press, 1910, xxx, 159, 320.

were a major article of trade in Surat. In these two years, merchants had little cloth to trade because the weavers were dead or had left their village or asked for high prices. The same thing happened with cart drivers. Even when food for humans was available, overland trade stopped because fodder was scarce. In the interior, 'the living [were] eating the dead', something Mundy described in graphic detail.

Famines tended to disperse artisans before they did the landed groups because their capital was portable and skills were widely valued. Europeans dealt with the weavers every day. During the 1630–31 Gujarat famine, foreign merchants needed to distribute food to keep the weavers in one place and get cloth woven by them.[31] On more than one occasion, they remarked on the hopeless inadequacy of the state authorities in dealing with relief and the aftermath.

The famine damaged the business of the Surat factory but did not stop it altogether. Some merchants survived, even if they struggled to provide food and water to the ships. Grain and dates came from Gombroon (Bandar Abbas), and rice from Masulipatnam, Bantam, and Comoro Islands.[32] The death of cart-drivers ensured that little of that rice went past the port town. The collapse of overland trade due to lack of supplies and transport stimulated short-haul coastal trade. The collapse of the Company's orders was an opportunity for private traders, with whom some Company officers had secret deals.

The Company's officers in Surat and Bantam made plans. From how the business developed after 1630, it seems that many officers thought it would be wiser to spread out, have more stations in the peninsular to reduce the risk of dying or at least staying unemployed in a famine, and explore Bengal. Bengal coarse silk and cotton were well-known articles in India-Europe and India-Southeast-Asia trade. More than that, Bengal was attractive for the low prices of food: 'extraordinary cheap sugar and other provisions of Bengal … very easily to be procured … thereby… to increase and support the constant mart for silk at Gombroon'.[33] The Bay of Bengal beyond Masulipatnam was unsafe because of the threat of Portuguese attack, though the English did try to explore the prospects since the 1620s. That changed somewhat in June 1632, with the expulsion of the Portuguese from Hooghly by Emperor Shah Jahan.

Erratic weather affected the area around Masulipatnam one or two years after the Gujarat famine and had a devastating impact on the trade passing

---

[31] William Moreland, *India at the Death of Akbar: An Economic Study*, London: Macmillan, 1920, 188.
[32] Foster, *The English Factories in India 1630–33*, 94, 145, 148, 178.   [33] Ibid.

through the port.[34] In the years immediately after, the English settled there and explored the prospects of trade to the north, closer to the mouth of the Hooghly River, and south, where Madras would come up shortly after. In 1633, an empty ship, the *Swan*, which had no trading prospect in Masulipatnam, was diverted towards Bengal. *Swan* was the third of three attempts to access the Bengal coast; the first two had to be abandoned because of cyclonic storms common in the Bay of Bengal. The *Swan* did not do much business but ended up in Balasore, where the Company established a base. With the start of a factory and fort in Madras, the move into Bengal became more promising.

A Study, In Contrast

The great attraction of Bengal was built on impressions of the lower Ganges Delta as a land where the cost of living was next to nothing because of abundant rain and water. The French voyager Francois Pyrard de Laval described Bengal (1607) as the rice bowl of southern Asia. The image stuck. After 1630, the image mattered more than ever.

Not much headway was made in building commercial access in the 1640s and the 1650s. The bases in western and southern India continued to function under uncertainty caused by climate. At the beginning of 1647, food was scarce, and the factors at Fort St. George in Madras wrote to their counter-parts in Masulipatnam for a supply of provisions, without which they expected to be reduced to a diet of rice and water. The mini-famine is also mentioned in a letter written at the same time to Surat, stating that it had 'almost destroyed all the kingdom', and there were losses of life in certain locations due to food scarcity.[35] However, coastal trade in rice was brisk, and some profit had been made by selling the rice from places outside the famine area.[36]

In the 1650s, the English factory records revealed almost constant anxiety over 'provisions'. More famines happened in the interior, in Malwa, Marwar, and Sind. If on a smaller scale than before, these disasters upset trade in Surat. Famines occurred in South India in 1659–62, 1675, and 1709–20, but apparently in regions that did not significantly affect trade and supplies to the European factories.[37] Still, concerns about food and famine had entered spatial policy.

---

[34] Sanjay Subrahmanyam, *The Political Economy of Commerce: Southern India 1500–1650*, Cambridge: Cambridge University Press, 1990, 333.

[35] William Foster, *The English Factories in India 1646–50*, Oxford: Clarendon Press, 1914, 70.

[36] Ibid., 163.

[37] F. R. Hemingway, *Madras District Gazetteers: Trichinopoly*, Madras: Government Press, 1907, 187.

Meanwhile, one major obstacle to expansion, Portuguese power, had begun to recede. The 1632 expulsion from Hooghly has been mentioned. In 1650, when Portuguese control over Muscat ended, a group of English officers were eager to step into their shoes. It is 'no hard thing', they petitioned the head office, 'to command this beneficial place with a relatively small force … that might keep the port and not only force the Persian to pay customs but also take customs of all junks at the mouth of the Gulf as the Portugal did'. The scheme, which essentially asked for a replication of the Portuguese policy of collecting protection money from shipping, ended with a sharp reproof from head office: 'we disown this your undertaking, it being contrary to that commission which we gave unto you … such a port as we intended must be … such a one that trade from India might be brought and drawn down to and also be able to defray its own charge.'[38] 'Defray own charge' meant mainly the ability to buy provisions and labour cheaply.

Not all seaboard places were alike by that benchmark. Muscat was given up mainly because its geography was too hostile for the trade expected. It was too dry, had too weak a monsoon, and had little local food trade. Gombroon or Bandar Abbas on the Persian Gulf was even drier. It had strategic advantages, but these came at a significant cost, as a Surat factor stranded in this port had explained in 1634: 'caused an undue outlay for food and water. The climate is very unwholesome …, never felt more heat in any part of the Indies'.[39] The 'foul weather and want of provisions' figured in other accounts of Gombroon in the seventeenth century when the English were interested in the town.[40]

Conditions worsened severely in 1658 when the Mughal succession wars broke out, causing the collapse of food trade over a vast area in the Deccan. The most consequential battle was fought in the Dharmat plains southwest of Ujjain in April 1658 between Aurangzeb and a coalition supporting his brother Dara Shikoh. The 50,000 combatants and perhaps an equal number of camp followers drained the countryside of food and disrupted north-west trade that passed through the area. The conflict moved towards northern India. Next year, the rains failed.

1661

In 1661, the East India Company headquarters wrote a letter to the officers at the Surat factory complaining that the latter were spending too much money on

---

[38] William Foster, *The English Factories in India 1655–60*, Oxford: Clarendon Press, 1921, 233, 321.

[39] William Foster, *The English Factories in India 1634–36*, Oxford: Clarendon Press, 1911.

[40] Foster, *The English Factories in India 1655–60*, 59.

food. 'When the gentlemen who advised you what the food cost should be', Surat officers replied, 'it might be a plentiful year. But the last two years have seen a great famine caused by little rain. Grain is dear. So are all other provisions. We do not feast'.[41]

For some time, news of a severe trade disruption was filtering in from Sind and Masulipatnam. The officers stationed there did not necessarily witness the disaster but were told about it. In Gujarat, provisions were dearer, 'but in [Sind] famine raged worse in any place, the living being hardly able to bury the dead'.[42] In September 1659, a letter from Sind said that the goods to be embarked at Lahribandar would be fewer than usual: 'the famine and plague in Sind is so great that it hath swept away most part of the people, and those that are left are few, and what they make is bought by the country merchant at any price.'[43]

The 1661 famine hit the Golconda state especially severely. Masulipatnam was a port that belonged to this state. 'We have at present', said the Masulipatnam factors a month later, 'so great a famine in these parts, the people dying daily for want of food, that we cannot have goods brought in as we expected'.[44] Around the port, 'want of rain the last year hath made all sorts of provisions to rise to double the price they use to be at. We fear the next year we shall not be able to send you any Agra goods; that place being now the seat of the war'.[45] Investing in saltpetre at 'Metchlepatam [was] altogether frustrated by the late famine that hath undone all the poor workmen'.[46] Like 1630, this was a three-year famine caused probably by an ENSO episode that led to a prolonged shortfall of rains. Wars imposed further disruption.

In the winter of 1668, a letter from Masulipatnam reported, 'a great fear of a famine in this place for want of rain, of which we have had none in a manner'. Rice sold at three times the normal rate. Cloth supplies were normal, but the workers to process these cloths for export could not be fed. 'We shall have them . . . go where they may find food.' Ultimately, the failure of the winter rains did not result in a full-scale famine that season, for the summer monsoon was a good one.[47]

Aftermath

In the middle decades of the seventeenth century, the English East India Company officers working in India displayed a growing awareness of the climatic conditions under which they operated, and the risks it posed to trade.

---

[41] Foster, *The English Factories in India 1661–64*, Oxford: Clarendon Press, 1923, 24.

[42] Foster, *The English Factories in India 1655–60*, 307.   [43] Ibid., 210.   [44] Ibid., 263.

[45] Ibid., 196.   [46] Foster, *The English Factories in India 1661–64*, 57.

[47] William Foster, *The English Factories in India 1668–1669*, Oxford: Clarendon Press, 1927, 152.

'In India, any failure of the rains, however restricted the area, was followed by famine and loss of life', said a letter in 1659.[48] The great famines were traumatic episodes, no doubt. Even milder but repeated droughts and the dependence on monsoon rains posed significant challenges for the East India merchants in procuring food and goods produced for export.[49]

Occasionally, European merchants and travellers reflected on how famines shaped Indian society. Famines in the arid tropical lands changed relationships between people. Even if people survived climatic shocks like floods and famines, they often ended up dependent on strangers and having to accept degrading inequality. Frequent famines in the ancient past drove 'aboriginals [to contract] away their freedom for bare but regular subsistence', said the maverick historian Damodar Kosambi. He was explaining the emergence of caste hierarchy relating it to India's geography.[50] European travellers in the sixteenth through the seventeenth century observed something similar happen before their eyes. Famines were an occasion that increased the supply of slaves. Chattel slavery was not common in any part of India, but the sale of children was familiar enough during famines. A Persian envoy of the sixteenth century took to Persia 'a large number of Indian children because famine had made them cheap during his visit. Duarte Barbosa tells us that when the people on the Coromandel coast were starving, the ships of Malabar would carry food there and return laden with slaves, the people selling their children for provisions'.[51]

Of more immediate concern was business strategy. The two famines strengthened the resolve of all Europeans to move away from the Surat-Masulipatnam axis. Surat and Masulipatnam were not great places from a climatic point of view. Generally speaking, the western coastal areas where the Europeans first settled down to trade were indirectly exposed to climatic risks. Gujarat had a coastal strip with fertile, well-watered land and an extensive hinterland that was semi-arid. Further south, coastal trading places were hemmed in by a long mountain range, and food, if not enough was available from coastal trade, came from beyond that range through passes. The famine of 1630 exposed the vulnerability of this geographical location, and the famine of 1661 revealed the additional risk of inland wars to food supplies to the coast.

Masulipatnam suffered a similar risk. Like Surat, the impact of inland famines on Coromandel was indirect but often severe. The Golconda state that owned Masulipatnam was in the pathway of a weak monsoon and exposed to high famine risks. Violent Bay of Bengal cyclone added to the problems of

---

[48] Foster, *The English Factories in India 1646–50*, 192.　　[49] Ibid., 89–90.

[50] Damodar Kosambi, *The Culture and Civilisation of Ancient India in Historical Outline*, London: Routledge and Kegan Paul, 1965, 88.

[51] Moreland, *India at the Death of Akbar: An Economic Study*, 92.

the place. S. Arasaratnam attributed the decline of English and Dutch engagement in Coromandel in the eighteenth century, among other factors, to the absence of adequate all-weather ports and destructive cyclonic storms.[52]

With improved knowledge the Europeans on the seaboard could weigh the costs and benefits of diversification. Since famines did not break out everywhere and were often local, diversification of bases would reduce the chances of food shortage in any one place. 'There is a necessity now', stated a letter from Fort St. George in 1659, 'of employing all places in these parts', for the continuance of the famine caused variations between places in their ability to get cloth woven.[53] These were difficult decisions. As the seventeenth century wore on, there was an increasing need for investment in defence. Spreading defence capacity thinly over a wide area would defeat the purpose. Further, though the coastline was thousands of miles long, few places could access a captive agricultural zone to serve the port with food, taxes, and labour.

The defence also had a food security dimension. Domestic politics threatened maritime trade by disrupting food supplies to the ports. The Mughal succession wars were a telling example. Bombay (which had started formally as a settlement in 1666) and Madras (1632–39) had a perennial problem with provisions. Neither place was within easy access to fertile croplands. Food merchants from outside the Company territory could be loyal to the Golconda or Maratha states. These trade channels followed politics. On numerous occasions, when there was a dispute with a local governor, the latter would try to stop the supply of provisions to the factory. Unlike in Bombay, where the British needed to negotiate with the Mughal governors, the Marathas, and the Sidis, and needed to outwit the Portuguese and the Dutch, diplomacy in Madras and Masulipatnam was bilateral. The Golconda state court was not easily accessible to the Europeans, so diplomacy often failed. 'The daily abuse of the governors of the poor' in Masulipatnam affected supplies of cloth and food to the factory, a 1658 letter complained.[54] Regular payment of tribute to the king kept things cordial. But with a change of ruler, the situation could become uncertain again. When negotiations stalled, the Golconda representatives would ask merchants to stop bringing food into Madras. One of the last such episodes occurred in 1681.[55]

---

[52] Arasaratnam, 'Factors in the Rise, Growth and Decline of Coromandel Ports CIRCA 1650-1720', 19–30.

[53] Foster, *The English Factories in India 1655–60*, 401–402.

[54] Foster, *The English Factories in India 1655–60*, 402.

[55] Charles Fawcett, *The English Factories in India, vol. 4 (New Series) The Eastern Coast and Bay of Bengal 1670–1677*, Oxford: Clarendon Press, 1955, lx.

Already, the second half of the seventeenth century saw diversifications away from the original hubs towards Bombay, Konkan, Balasore, Malabar, Godavari Delta, and Bengal. Of these places, Bombay struggled to become a trading hub. Too many things were going wrong there. Madras functioned more as a defence post than a trading post. The Konkan settlements did not show much promise. Trading prospects were more promising with Malabar, Balasore, Godavari Delta, and Bengal. The common factor between all four places was cheap food and plentiful water.

The drive towards Bengal derived from knowledge of trade routes and Bengal's riparian access to North India, but also powerfully from the knowledge that of all regions of India, Bengal had the lowest food costs and almost no history of famine. Eventually, when Calcutta was established (around 1690), food came from local markets and croplands, and the supply did not depend on long-distance traders from a potentially hostile land.

Conclusion

The section's key message is that famines most starkly illustrate the natural advantages of the seaboard. These episodes also sharpened the geographical awareness of European merchants in India, which left a legacy.

The tropical monsoon climate entailed a high risk of drought and famine, which, in extreme cases, led to rebellion and state collapse. The seaboard in the South Asian landmass had, by and large, a more benign climate and, thanks to the access to deltaic rivers, could survive droughts better. The great western Indian famine of 1630 had an asymmetric impact on the interior and the seaboard. From that point onward, if not earlier, the cost of 'provisions' became a benchmark for locational decisions and the decision to nurture some places over others.

As the seventeenth century ended, the officers managing the diversification could see that the strategy cost money and imposed huge coordination costs. The effort to spread resources too thinly was not sensible and had created settlements vulnerable to new uncertainties. In 1679, the Madras Agent Streynsham Master toured the factories on the east coast. He travelled from Madras to Hooghly on horseback or boats and visited every factory on the way. Master was a highly able administrator; his bosses feared he was too independent-minded to follow instructions. The tour aimed to bring order into a disorganized system. Accounts were badly maintained with cash missing, officers spent more time hunting boars than doing business (Thomas Labrun was carried off by a tiger while hunting near Balasore), everywhere 'freemen' or private traders roamed, some had borrowed from the factory, and these debts were going bad. The Patna agent Job Charnock never answered letters.[56] The letters ordered him to leave Patna. He refused to read them and did not leave Patna.

This chaotic diversification left a legacy, nevertheless. By the mid eighteenth century, the English Company and most of its rivals had entrenched themselves in Bengal and Malabar, the two most resource-rich regions of India. These two locations would serve commerce and shape politics, as we see in Section 3.

3 Forging Connections in the Eighteenth Century

Exploring further the idea that places matter, this section will describe a concentration of the British East India Company's enterprise towards the two most resource-secure places, Bengal and Malabar. There was a difference between the two. In Bengal, the gateway to the Indo-Gangetic Basin, the Company built connections with merchants and bankers engaged in overland trade through trading in the interior. Malabar commercial operations were of a smaller scale, but the region became critical with the emergence of Mysorean power, and then, given its geography, access to overland routes began to matter.

Of the three port towns where the Company was a territorial power in the mid eighteenth century, the position of both Bombay and Madras was particularly insecure. Neither city was vital to trading operations nor had deep links with overland trade. The Company's Malabar and Bengal activity was different. In the mid eighteenth century, both places were becoming politically more significant. Both places had a concentration of merchants. And in both, it was obvious that dealing with the local states from a position of power would also strengthen positions in the market. Connections forged between overland and the seaboard were critical to commerce and politics. Nowhere else were these connections so consequential as in Bengal and Malabar.

The three areas in India where a British East India Company state formed in the second half of the eighteenth century – Bengal, Malabar, and the Eastern Deltas – had somewhat different histories. The Deltas were a gift, but one whose potential value many Company officers understood from their trading past. Elsewhere, trade figured more directly. In Bengal, it figured in the shape of alliances. In Malabar, it figured as a partnership. In both cases, knowledge of the land had developed through a fifty-year experience of trying to access the overland. In Bengal, the river was crucial for that process. In Malabar, mountain passes were the key.

---

[56] Richard Temple, ed., *Diaries of Streynsham Master (1675–1680)*, 2 vols., London: John Murray, 1911.

Post-Diversification

In the second half of the seventeenth century, European commercial enterprises in India were diversifying their bases. The Portuguese moved from western Bengal towards the eastern Bengal delta, the Dutch established a bond with the king of Cochin, and the English went to Konkan.

In the 1650s, the English East India Company had factories in Surat, Ahmedabad, Agra, and Thatta (Sind) in India, Gombroon and Ispahan in Persia. These were administered from Surat, which was called a presidency. Those under the Madras president were Fort St. George and Masulipatnam, Balasore, Hooghly, Bantam in Java, and at least four in Southeast Asia, including Sumatra, Macassar in the Celebes, and Pegu. After reconstitution of the Company in 1657, all eastern establishments came under one President and Council seated at Surat. There were four branches under the presidency, the Coromandel Coast, Bengal, Persia, and Bantam (Java), each under an agent and a council. The Bengal agent supervised Hooghly, Patna, and Kasimbazar; the agent at Madras supervised Masulipatnam, Petapoli, and Viravasaram. Persia's administrative structure was unclear, though the Gombroon factory continued functioning. The Surat office oversaw Ahmedabad, Thatta, and in Konkan, Rajapur. The Company's operations in North India did not figure prominently in this replanning.

The administrative structure with top-down authority created more problems than they solved. Because of communication difficulties, delays in transit, and the virtual impossibility of moving money between stations, the branches were effectively independent. Some places pulled a lot more weight than others. In the 1660s, the East India Company owned territory in Bombay, and that move promised to change the structure. The officers understood the place could one day become a hub of Arabian Sea trade, connecting India, Persia, the Red Sea, and Africa. Contemporary factory records mention the desire to have ships go from Bombay to Persia and the Red Sea and to encourage merchants to inhabit the area.[57] But in practical terms, Bombay's commercial future was uncertain. As the administrators of Bombay realized, the place had very poor road access to the Deccan. Gerald Aungier, the governor of Bombay, committed to building a viable town economy from scratch thought that a network of settlements on the western coast sending goods to Bombay would solve this problem. Broach in the north and Dharangaon, Rajapur, and Karwar in the south might serve this purpose. Further south, Calicut and Baliapatam were also part of the plan to diversify from hubs to networks. Baliapatam proved too uneconomical and was dissolved (Figure 3). The Company's interest in the Konkan littoral partly stemmed from this vision.

---

[57] William Foster, *The English Factories in India 1668–69*, Oxford: Clarendon Press, 1927, 17–18, 57.

Figure 3 Baliapatam, William Daniell. One of dozens of trading stations the East India Company established and then merged with other stations. At the time of the painting (early nineteenth century), the Baliapatam factory had been abandoned for decades.

Source: Alamy, public domain image.

Although Broach did better, none of the Konkan ports had a happy career. With conflicts raging in the Deccan, little trade passed through them. There were occasional raids by Maratha commanders. Rajapur had definite promise as an Arabian Sea port. A few local merchants from Malabar engaged in the spice trade and supplied goods to the English factory at Gombroon. However, too little money and effort went into the infrastructure here, and the Company had difficulty building a factory and strengthening the defence of its base.

In the eastern seaboard, the British would need to deal with the political elite governing the Mughal province, Bengal, and Portuguese raiders on the mouth of the Hooghly. Both were complex challenges. In this scenario, one place above all gained prominence.

Towards Balasore

The Mughal incorporation of Orissa did not significantly change most of the smaller polities ruling the region, except for a strip of land near the sea where some of the largest commercial towns were located. Initially included in the

Bengal suba or province, this seaboard became more closely integrated with the economy of Bengal, possibly to the detriment of ports further south.

European commercial settlements in this area started in 1514, with a few Portuguese traders arriving in Pipli. The place was located, as nearly every other, on a delta (Subarnarekha) with access to villages that produced textiles. By the time the English and the Dutch became interested in the area, the 1630s, the river was silting. The English East India Company had established a factory at Balasore in the early 1630s, but following a dispute with the local authorities, they abandoned the factory in 1633. Abandoning Bengal was not really an option. After that, Hariharpur nearby was used as a base to conduct trade with Bengal for some time.

After trying a few other seaboard places, the principal one, Hariharpur, became unattractive due to the silting of rivers. European interest concentrated on Balasore, on the delta of the Budhabalang River. The years between 1632 and 1660 were significant in this enterprise because of the Gujarat famine. The epicentre of the 1630 and 1661 famines were in western India, but for reasons not entirely clear, they had a severe impact on the south-eastern seaports like Ganjam and Masulipatnam, inducing the English and the Dutch to relocate business and settlement further north. The English, Dutch, Danish merchants, and the French would arrive at Balasore at different points between 1660 and 1700. The English made a more serious commitment to the place, mainly because the Dutch had a secure hold over the Bengal trade.

Like Surat, on a considerably smaller scale and briefer period, Balasore drew in North Indian merchants, who appeared as agents and contractors of the European companies and induced the local rulers and their governors to operate their own trading business on the side.[58] Cowries from the Maldives were a dominant interest among the merchants connected to governance. The most prominent merchant firms, Chintaman Shah and Khem Chand, were not exclusively agents. They had a diversified business in which products from Southeast Asia figured. All ports on the eastern seaboard made extensive coastal trade in grain. The chief broker for the English Company in 1670, Khem Chand, was described as the chief merchant, meaning that his business was already established when he took the agency of the Company. In that very profitable role, Khem Chand could never rest easy. Sources suggest that he was squeezed between two masters, the governor who constantly harassed him for money and the Company who found his loyalty questionable.

---

[58] Patit Paban Mishra, 'Balasore Port-Town in Seventeenth Century', *Proceedings of the Indian History Congress*, 59, 1998, 301–310.

Balasore was potentially a seaport and a market where cloths from weaver villages in Soro, Hariharpur, and Mohanpur would be sent for sale to merchants. The chief among these products were sannoe (sanu, sanna), plain white (sometimes blue) cotton fabrics, and ginghams, dyed cotton fabrics. The place had good road connections with these sources. For the English, it was relatively safe from interference by rival Portuguese and Dutch. The governor of the place wanted European trading settlements. He received tribute in money in return.

Balasore was a small market relative to Hooghly or Masulipatnam, but it had unique advantages. One that was unmatched by any other place on the Bay of Bengal was access to wild silks (tusser) from the Mayurbhanj kingdom to the northwest. Balasore was connected with Hooghly and Dhaka via a short journey by sea and river. But the real worth of the place was its proximity to Bengal, and possibly access to Burma and Thailand. Some Bengal products came to Balasore. The Company would use the idle shipping during the post-monsoon months to conduct trade with Bengal and Persia. The governor of the place, landlords, and the Mughal ruler wanted elephants from Southeast Asia, some of which came to Balasore. Again, seasonally idle shipping came in handy. With timber available from forests to the northwest and rivers connecting these sources with the coast, ship repairs and even shipbuilding could develop in and near the town.

Balasore had disadvantages, too, quite serious ones. Although a short journey away from Bengal, it was not easy to navigate through the sandbanks of the mouth of the Hooghly. The Company had to invite trained pilots to settle in Balasore and take the ships to Hooghly.[59] The place was not suitable for big ships, which had to anchor miles away at the end of a route known as the Balasore Road, part of which was quite dangerous to navigate. After Emperor Shah Jahan drove the Portuguese out of Hooghly in 1632, small bands of Portuguese settlers and Arakan pirates would raid ships in the northern part of the Bay of Bengal. For the Mughal governor Shaista Khan, suppressing piracy was a major preoccupation in the 1660s. He was not very successful without an effective navy. Europeans, therefore, needed to invest money in their defence.

The politics of Balasore was unstable. Balasore passed between the Bengal and Orissa administrations several times, and the local governor had a great deal of autonomy and power throughout. Although the Europeans obtained trade licenses from the provincial courts, the governor's expectations, interests, and inclinations mattered to business continuity. In turn, the Europeans and Indian

---

[59] Foster, *The English Factories in India 1668–69*, x.

merchants often tried to manipulate candidacy for the governorship, an office that was auctioned, without much success. Every new governor tried to recoup the money paid for the post by insisting on a new license to trade exchanged for cash. Politically, Balasore was on the fringes of the Mughal Empire rather than being central in the way Hooghly was. The emperor and the Bengal governor did not have a cordial relationship with the kings and chiefs who controlled extensive territory in interior Orissa and regulated the import of goods, including lead and elephants from Southeast Asia and guns from Europe. These embargos and the poor saleability of English broadcloth compromised the Balasore merchants' ability to obtain textiles on behalf of the English Company.

As the historian Jagadish Narayan Sarkar said, obtaining finance in Balasore was a constant worry.[60] Most transactions in local markets used the small denomination cowrie shell. The local banking was not as well developed as in Surat, and interest rates were high. It seems that the Bay of Bengal and India-Southeast-Asia trade generally suffered with the cessation of Japanese silver flows from the east to the west. European merchants developed access to American silver in response, but that West-to-East flow ended up in the more prominent centres of operations and bypassed the smaller ports. In Balasore, the English struggled to sell broadcloth.

The Company officers could not contract with the weavers bypassing the merchants and had to accept a loss by way of interest. Contract failure was frequent and damaging. One curious outcome of this difficulty was the emergence of rampant violation of the charter by individual officers. Private traders who established personal connections with the merchants were better off, and officers used that opportunity perhaps more in Balasore than anywhere else.

Balasore never quite took off. From the start of a serious interest in the place, some officers thought the Company was stretching its investment too thin. Jonathan Trevisa, a Balasore chief, thought it would be best to reduce the number of factories in eastern India. The place was becoming unsustainable 'in view of the small amount of business done by the English and the disturbed state of the country'. When Trevisa said this, the ruler of the place had a dispute with the English and tried to blockade English trade. An alternative plan 'in future [was for] their ships would come up the river to [Hooghly], as was the practice of the Dutch'.[61]

Nothing much came of the move in the 1650s. Trevisa's successor Blake thought that 'there is an absolute necessity of keepeing Ballasore'.[62] Ten years later, the proposal to abandon returned. Some considered the Balasore factory to be

---

[60] Jagadish Narayan Sarkar, 'Notes on Balasore and the English in the First Half of the Seventeenth Century', *Proceedings of the Indian History Congress*, 13, 1950, 209–221.
[61] Foster, *English Factories in India 1661–4*, 401.   [62] Ibid., 401.

unnecessary and expensive. '[T]he Bay business [will be brought] into some decorum if it would be possible to contrive all shipping henceforward to go up directly for Hooghly. This would help the company save the expenses incurred annually in transporting the goods from Hooghly to Ballasore Road.'[63] Again, no decision to give up on Balasore was possible for at least twenty more years, even as the English increased their presence in Bengal. The English Company continued their troubled negotiations to gain a secure place in Hooghly in the 1680s. To their annoyance, the Dutch were already a partner of the Bengal government in expeditions against the Portuguese. Balasore, therefore, remained in a key position.

The problem of Balasore was not political only. It was geographical. Accessing river trade required relying on country boats and navigators. Their cooperation was not assured. The climate of the Bay of Bengal, which produced powerful storms in two seasons in the year, was not easy to negotiate for seventeenth-century ships. In 1664, a monsoon storm damaged a large number of country boats. Ships (like the Hope in 1661) going from Masulipatnam to Bengal and Balasore to Bengal were driven by 'fierce winds' off course. The 1661 cyclone was huge, destroying many boats in the port: 'no less than 22 junks and vessels hath bin cast away'.[64] On the 12th of October 1663, there was another 'great storm in the Bay Bengal'. The accompanying tsunami forced a ship miles inshore, 'where she lyeth in the mud so that boats cannot come at her, and they fear past recovery'.[65] The next year, overland trade failed because a storm had destroyed many country boats, and the Nawab requisitioned the others.

Even in the normal monsoon season, 'the violent rain and overflowing much obstruct the procure of goods (which are not made in town, but at a considerable distance) by the dangerous . . . transportation'.[66] The passage from the Balasore Road into the town in small boats was challenging to navigate. Freshly arrived Englishmen were at the mercy of the boatmen. On one occasion, the boatmen quietly diverted the course to arrive at a small village. The starving passengers received a warm welcome there and were fed very well. While they were taking a well-earned nap, the goods were stolen by the hosts and the boatmen. 'The Governor took the part of the boatmen and contrived the escape of some of the chief offenders.'[67]

Not surprisingly, the Company's presence in the place notwithstanding, there was never enough investment in it. In the 1670s, the Balasore factory looked like a decent building only from a distance. Inside was a decrepit collection of mud huts, each 'dark, low, and moist'. Goods were damaged, and there was a pervasive mood of insecurity.[68]

---

[63] Ibid., 66. [64] Foster, *The English Factories in India 1661–4*, 145. [65] Ibid., 176.
[66] Foster, *The English Factories in India 1668–69*, 304. [67] Ibid., 312. [68] Ibid., 305.

Towards Bengal

One of the main attractions of Bengal was the cheap riparian highway that connected it with the Indo-Gangetic Basin, from where came sugar, indigo, and saltpetre. The northern and eastern half of the Bay of Bengal joined the Bengal delta with Burma, Indonesia, the Malaya, and China. The trans-Himalayan overland trade joined the Bay of Bengal trade with China and Tibet.

In 1651, a small team moved north from Balasore to negotiate with the Mughal provincial authorities and set up a factory at Hooghly. The business of trade in silk and saltpetre was profitable. But European rivalry was fierce. The factory paid large sums of money to local governors (*zamindars*) as bribes. The money brought some advantages. In turn, the local government furnished troops and artisans with which to build houses and stores when it was desired to move the factory to a new location, as it was at Kasimbazar.[69] The uneasy relationship continued into the 1660s and beyond, as new agreements were drawn with the governor of Bengal. The factors stationed at Hooghly constantly criticized the poor infrastructure of the town, the free enterprise of private merchants flouting the Company's charter, and the difficulty of dealing with the local elite even when an army of interpreters was hired for the job.

And yet, Bengal was too attractive a place to give up on. All European agents agreed on that point, and by the end of the seventeenth century, the British, the Danes, and the Dutch had been joined by the French. About this time, François Bernier wrote his famous lines on Bengal: 'The rich exuberance of the country, together with the beauty and amiable disposition of the native women, has given rise to a proverb in common use among the Portuguese, English, and Dutch, that the Kingdom of Bengale has a hundred gates open for entrance, but not one for departure.'[70]

Around 1687, Job Charnock, an officer and the temporary chief of the Company's station in Bengal, obtained permission from the province's ruler to create a settlement on the Hooghly River. The decision did not reflect great prescience. It was just another settlement among many. Two accidental factors, the 1740s European War (1740–60), which pitted the French against the English in Bengal and the Maratha incursions into western Bengal that drove many Bengali businesses and service workers to Calcutta, showed that Calcutta had been a good strategic investment. This history will appear in full detail in the next section.

---

[69] Bimala Prasad Mukherji, 'The English Factory at Hooghly (1651–1690)', *Proceedings of the Indian History Congress*, 19, 1956, 290–300.

[70] François Bernier, *Travels in the Mogul Empire AD 1656–1668*, London: Humphrey Milford, 1916, 439.

Towards Malabar

In the seventeenth century, the British arrived on the Malabar Coast and founded a factory and trading station in Tellicherry in north Malabar (1694, Figure 4). In the same decade, a factory came up further south in Anjengo. Kings in this part were generally keen to form alliances with the Europeans to earn easy money from commissions on selling spices. The actual business was done between the Mappilah or Moplah merchants who procured the goods and the European trading companies. Pepper was grown in territories of Nair landlords in the interior.

In the 1750s, the East India Company was a dominant player in the pepper trade from Malabar. No other European rivals could match their business. The rise to dominance was not owed to political or military power. The Company did maintain a friendly relationship with the local rulers, the Nair chieftain of the Kolathiri kingdom in North Malabar, but that relationship was mediated more by financial advantages than military power. Partnerships with merchants mattered more.

In the seventeenth century, the Dutch and the English took a share of the lucrative spices trade. Portuguese influence along the Malabar coast declined in

Figure 4 Tellicherry. Print commissioned by East India Company in 1732.
Source: Yale Center of British Art, public domain image.

the 1660s following a war with the Dutch. The Dutch had a foothold in Ponnani, a seaboard town on the border of Cochin and Calicut. With Portuguese defeat in 1663, the Dutch came to control a string of seaboard towns, the most crucial for trade being Cochin. The kingdom of Cochin was a militarily weak power, sharing that limited power with regional warlords. Dutch protection was necessary for its survival. After that, Ponnani lost its economic significance, and having secured a partnership with the king of Cochin, the Dutch, the dominant partner, lost interest in the rest of the western seaboard.

Mahe was established around 1720 and became the centre of French colonial administration and commercial activities on the Malabar coast. Its location provided easier accessibility to the pepper-growing areas. The co-existence with the English factory just across the Kuyyali River added an element of instability. But Mahe survived because of its strategic importance. It was the recruiting centre for soldiers and a place where intelligence from Europe came before it reached Pondicherry.[71]

The Company's success in the seaboard lay elsewhere than their muscle power. It rested on the way it encouraged local trading enterprise. Wherever they governed places, the Company encouraged markets, for the tax collected on local trade met a part of the costs of police and security. Tellicherry bazaar, where Malabar commodities and imported commodities from different markets of the world were sold in separate shops, had grown in the early eighteenth century. Skilled labourers like weavers, carpenters, and smiths were essential members of the bazaar system. The Company invited people proficient in several languages to settle and act as interpreters in dealings with merchants and local rulers. As trade grew, so did trade credit and moneylending. The money-changing business flourished as well. The Muslim merchants were not the only intermediaries between the Company and the growers. The ethnic composition was mixed, with Hindu and Jewish firms present alongside the Mappilahs, and it was a competitive field.[72] These southern ports developed their own trading interest around pepper and were never satellites of Bombay or Madras.

The eighteenth-century situation in Malabar was not particularly cordial. The British complained bitterly about the unreliability of supplies, the disloyalty of the contractors, and the Calicut Zamorin's constant demand for 'loans'. It turned out that one factor above all was responsible for these troubles: Dutch

---

[71] Joy Varkey, 'The Significance of Mahe in Eighteenth-Century French India', *Proceedings of the Indian History Congress*, 58, 1997, 295–302.

[72] M. Arun Thomas, 'Merchants, Markets and Merchandise: Strategy of English East India Company Trade in Tellicherry 1725–1750', PhD Dissertation of the University of Calicut, 2015.

intrigue. Still, none of the European trading firms faced an existential threat in Malabar.

Towards the Eastern Deltas

The areas in the Coromandel where European business tended to go were the Godavari, Krishna, and Kaveri Deltas. On the Coromandel coast in the 1680s, the Company was setting up new factories, with six places besides Madras dominating the network: Petapole, Conimere, Cuddalore, Vizagapatam, Madapollam, and Masulipatnam. Conimere, thirteen miles north of Pondicherry, was abandoned in 1698. Shortly before, settlements at Cuddalore and Porto Novo had shifted to Conimere. Madapollam was a weaving village on the delta of the Godavari, which ceased to be crucial from sometime in the early eighteenth century. Petapole (Petapoli or Peddapalli) was in the Krishna River delta. Little is known about the Vizagapatam settlement except that the officers in charge there fought bitterly with each other. When negotiations with the Nizam on protection began in the late eighteenth century, these areas, the Northern Circars, changed hands and became one of the earliest regions to be owned by the Company.

The Godavari and Krishna Deltas evoked a particular interest among private traders. The local chiefs and warlords were weak, so negotiations were easier here, and the partnership with Company officers went unnoticed. Once again, food security was prominent in their concerns. John Smythe, a private trader, wrote about Viravasaram, praising the place enthusiastically, complaining only of the heat: 'The chiefest thing needful is a good hat.' Other than that, the country is 'a very cheap place of residence, were it not for the .. multiplicity of servants we strangers are constrained to keep; all men being respected according to his train and habit. ... All sorts of provisions are extreme cheap'.[73] Viravasaram did not emerge as a major trading hub, it is difficult to know why. One possible factor was that the Company was unwilling to invest enough money in acquiring land and building infrastructure there.

The extensive operation of the private traders and 'interlopers' who preferred to work from small and poorly governed ports was one reason the expansion was becoming unsustainable and unmanageable for the Company's head office. Madapollam and Peddapalli were weaving villages with extensive supply capacity, but neither was a town. There were few individuals there with enough political power to negotiate with. That suited the private traders and the Company employees in Masulipatnam who routinely diverted a part of the investment funds to these places for their private trade. That made it difficult for the Company to relocate operations officially

---

[73] Foster, *The English Factories in India 1655–60*, 261.

to these places. In the early eighteenth century, there was a definite trend to concentrate efforts in Madras.

Malabar and the Eastern Deltas were ruled by small states and warlords. Kingdoms in this region were often engaged in military contests without sufficient fiscal strength to form effective armies. In that scenario, all had an interest in earning money from trade, and Indo-European trade came as a convenient opportunity. If one small kingdom entered a negotiation with a European firm, others rushed in from fear of falling behind in financial advantage. That eagerness to partner with the Europeans did not rest on unequal power but on the relatively weak fiscalism of all regional states.

An early instance of this process was the 'Pulicat enterprise'. Pulicat became a major centre of Dutch trade on the Coromandel in the seventeenth century. The enterprise refers to the Dutch East India Company's (VOC) mission to the courts of Chandragiri and Senji through two brothers, who were powerful, semi-independent figures engaged in revenue-farming, inland trade, and maritime trade, as well as military activity. The enterprise contained Portuguese influence in the court and helped in negotiations with other warlords inland.[74] Later in the seventeenth and early eighteenth century, a similar contest would appear in Malabar that helped the British East India Company to forge strong relationships with indigenous chiefs and merchants there.

S. Arasaratnam discusses the policies and attitudes of the rulers of Madura, Ramnad, and Tanjore towards trade in the southern Indian coast in the second half of the seventeenth century.[75] The rulers were interested in preserving their independence from Islamic powers to the north and from each other but also actively pursued commercial policies to secure their share in the trade of the coastal area. By the end of the century, each of these powers had a treaty with the Dutch that made considerable commercial, extra-territorial, and even political concessions to the latter. The Dutch aimed to control the entry and exit points and the major traded commodities.

Connections with Inland

Throughout the seventeenth century and well into the eighteenth, the Europeans forged partnerships with indigenous merchants. Some of that relationship stemmed from commodities that traded overland and where overland merchant groups were already entrenched – indigo, silk, saltpetre, pepper, sugar, for example. Partly, it was owed to deals the companies struck with urban bankers.

---

[74] Sanjay Subrahmanyam, 'The "Pulicat Enterprise": Luso-Dutch Conflict in South-eastern India, 1610–1640', *South Asia: Journal of South Asian Studies*, 9(2), 1986, 17–36.

[75] S. Arasaratnam, 'The Politics of Commerce in the Coastal Kingdoms of Tamil Nad 1650–1700', *South Asia: Journal of South Asian Studies*, 1(1), 1971, 1–19.

A third strategy can be called the 'bazaar strategy'. If the authorities controlled land beyond the shipping yard, they invited settlers and set up bazaars. If not agricultural taxes, taxes from markets would balance the budget of governing the places. More discussion on the bazaar strategy will come later.

One universal element in this game in South India was the broker, agent, interpreter, and indigenous merchants, prominent in the local chiefs' courts. Their incentive to represent European interests was based on money and the prospect of using European transport and institutional infrastructure to advance their business interest. There was no direct military or political interest in how these relationships unfolded in the seventeenth century.

Madras was located close to a fertile agricultural tract to its southwest. But, this area was not a secure 'hinterland' in the seventeenth century. References to markets abound, so do references to the difficulties of obtaining supplies and, occasionally, deliberate obstructions. Undoubtedly, Fort St. George was becoming important as a port of call for Asian merchants. Coastal trade in the Bay of Bengal circulated crucial provisions and major and minor exportable goods. Indigenous merchants operated these trades, without which the Madras economy would collapse.[76] But this advantage receded somewhat in the eighteenth century.

European factors stationed at Surat grumbled about the decrease in shipping from the town in the 1720s and 1730s. Maratha invasions in Gujarat caused disruptions to the town's supply of food, textiles, and tax money. Moreover, disagreements among merchants ran the risk of blowing up under the town's collapsing government. Merchants united under the banner of their local communities or took sides with the empire or the local governor.

This turmoil ultimately led the British to relocate their fleet to the safer port of Bombay. The town's economic hinterland shrank in size as Mughal authority over Surat disintegrated, and local political actors were left without effective top-down control. The likelihood of conflicts between Europeans and Indians grew, leading the Europeans to shut the port repeatedly. The Company occupied the port in 1759. Whether the occupation followed a partnership or a dispute between commercial interests is debatable. In any case, Bombay overtook Surat in the second half of the twentieth century, even though Surat remained relevant.[77]

In Surat, the Parsis were the only community without a choice but to support the English. They did not form a coherent business community in the way the Hindu and Muslim seafaring merchants did. Most Parsis were carpenters,

---

[76] Radhika Seshan, 'Coastal Connections of Fort St. George (Madras/Chennai) in the 17th Century', *Proceedings of the Indian History Congress*, 78, 2017, 372–379.

[77] Lakshmi Subramanian, *Indigenous Capital and Imperial Expansion: Bombay, Surat and the West Coast*, New Delhi: Oxford University Press, 1996.

farmers, and orchard owners. A handful of them in the western coast had a history of partnership with the Company, even though these contracts occasionally failed. In the harsh climate of the 1730s, the Company benefited from the possibility of wider commercial alliances with the Parsis. Bombay's access to lumber from the Malabar jungles was a decisive advantage over Surat. Bombay was in a better location to manufacture ships. Several weavers and carpenters from Surat moved to Bombay. The shipbuilding business that the Parsi carpenters recreated eclipsed Surat shipping. The Company hired master shipbuilder Lowji Wadia as its principal contractor in the 1740s to build and repair its ships. Meanwhile, the timber contract belonged to three more Parsi merchant households.

In Calcutta, the bazaar strategy was active and received an impetus when the Maratha raids forced many moneyed people to flee the western borders of Bengal and resettle in Calcutta. Even before that, the Ganges River traffic had permitted the British to build ties with the North Indian merchants and bankers. These ties played a critical role during the mid eighteenth-century political transition in Bengal. Around then, the Marathas of western and central India had emerged as India's most formidable military force. The Maratha force was divided into clans and regions. One of these raided western Bengal seeking to capture a part of Bengal's taxes. These raids drained the Bengal treasury and the military capacity of the state. When the young Nawab Sirajuddaula succeeded to the throne, the affairs of the state were in chaos, and infighting was rife in the court. The Company, with its base in the well-defended Calcutta port, appeared immune to the turmoil. Merchants from western Bengal fled to its protection and built ties with European merchants. As the Maratha threat receded, the Company's power and its meddling in the affairs of the state alarmed the Nawab, making a showdown inevitable.

The Company's head office in the City of London had neither full knowledge of what was happening in Bengal nor the power to control its officers. Instead, a series of local circumstances and accidents combined to shape the transfer of power between 1757 and 1765. Siraj's chaotic invasion of Calcutta, the damaging legacy of the Maratha raids, Robert Clive's ambitions, Anglo-French rivalry, help from the Royal Navy, traitors in the court, and efficient use of artillery power in the decisive Battle of Plassey saw a small coterie of officers take charge of the revenues of several districts of Bengal (1757). Eight years later, the Mughal king formally conceded power over a large swathe of eastern India to the Company.

The arrangement between the Nawab of the Bengal province (subah) and the Company was purely based on a promise of military service against a share in the revenue to meet the costs of a standing force and make for losses should a conflict break out. Mir Zafar, who took over as the Nawab, was widely regarded as incompetent to govern. In 1760, fearing a conspiracy against him, he ordered his henchmen to eliminate several court officers and surviving members of the past Nawab Alivardi Khan's family. More threatening still, troops had received no pay, and the big landlords on the west and south of the capital were arming themselves for a potential attack.[78] By then, the British East India Company had managed to build a sizeable infantry army, though it was doubtful if it could stand up to a coalition of forces in the rest of India. With that resource in hand, the Company coerced Mir Zafar to give up power. A fresh agreement was secured by a treaty that precisely demarcated civil administration in which the Company would have no say, and the military affairs, in which it would have a part to play. The agreement was drawn between the new ruler Mir Kasim and Henry Vansittart, the chief officer in Bengal in 1764. When that agreement soured, a wider confrontation was inevitable.

Of all the places where the British Empire began in the eighteenth century, only in Malabar did the Company's army fight its way to a conquest of territorial power. Even so, this was not a story of military strategy. Trade here, as in Bengal but in a different way, had made the knowledge of trade routes more accessible. During the third and fourth Anglo-Mysore Wars, troops on the winning side targeted holding these routes and made the crucial difference.

'India Is Ours'

Thus said General George Harris, the commander in chief of the Company's army, at the end of the fourth Anglo-Mysore war. The bare facts of the thirty-year-long conflict that ended with British pre-eminence over South India are too well-known to deserve a detailed restatement. Briefly, the context for these conflicts was the rivalry between three major military forces in the 1760s: the Mysore warlord Hyder Ali, who commanded a cavalry and set up a small navy; the Maratha forces under the Peshwa of Pune; and the British East India Company, which had by then created an infantry army, though divided between camps in different places. Other prominent kingdoms were on the western coast, the mountains, and the eastern seaboard, but none militarily consequential. The same can be said of the Nizam of Hyderabad, the French in Mahe and Pondicherry, and the Dutch based in Cochin and Pulicat. The three main military forces distrusted each other and feared each other. Mysore wanted to control Malabar to gather more revenue. The British feared this would be the end of Tellicherry. The Nizam feared that his territory would be the next. The Marathas saw the situation as a chance to extract protection money from

---

[78] Robert Clive et al. *Reflections on the Present Commotion in Bengal*, London: J. Kearsly, 1764.

the Nizam. Mysore feared the Marathas and resented that the British did not offer help.

The first of the four Anglo-Mysore wars was fought between Hyder Ali and the Nizam of Hyderabad, with the Company as the latter's ally. That military alliance formed after an earlier alliance between the Nizam and Ali had soured. The conflicts in 1768 saw Ali at the gates of a defenceless Madras, forcing the British to enter a peace treaty. The second Anglo-Mysore war (1780–83) started with the British capture of Mahe, an effect of the Revolutionary War in America. Hyder Ali, the protector of the French, stepped in. He died during the conflict, but his son Tipu Sultan (Tippoo Sultan in the British sources) signed a treaty. Nothing much changed in territorial control. The Third War (1790–92) began with Tipu Sultan's expansion into Malabar and Travancore, British allies. The war ended with a significant loss of Mysore territory, including control over crucial roads that connected the landlocked state with the western seaboard. The fourth and final war (1799) followed Napoleon's mission to Tipu Sultan, proposing a joint front, and the latter's positive response. The attack led to Tipu Sultan's death and the fall of the capital.

These wars are well-known. Yet there is a great scarcity of material on crucial military logistics. Reports sent from the frontline tend to be glorified accounts of the valour of individual officers and are too scanty on crucial organizational questions. How were the armies supplied? How did they move over long distances? In the battles between the British and the Mysore warlords, Mysore fielded a stronger cavalry than the British did. In contrast, the latter had the advantage of a more disciplined infantry and control of the seas.[79] The soldiers needed to be camped, fed, and supplied with ammunition. Having a secure base on a trade route was crucial to that effort. How was that achieved?

The tide turned in 1790, not because the British had a more powerful army or stronger allies but because their entrenched position on the western and eastern seaboards had enabled them to secure control over the most important conduit for moving goods and people. This was the Palghat gap, a forty-mile-wide pass through the Western Ghats. One base mattered above all, and this was the Palghat fort. When hostilities broke out in 1798–99, Mysore had lost access to the two crucial roads that linked the seaboard with the inland through the otherwise impassable Western Ghat. Men and equipment moved more freely along these roads, giving the British a vital advantage.

We must step back from military action and look towards trade on the western seaboard to see how that advantage went to the Company's army. The emergence

---

[79] Pradeep P. Barua, 'Maritime Trade, Seapower, and The Anglo-Mysore Wars, 1767–1799', *The Historian*, 73(1), 2011, 22–40.

of Mysore as the most militaristic state in southern India upset the commercial stability on the western seaboard in two ways. It drove a wedge between the French in Mahe and the British in Tellicherry, the former being collaborators and partners of Hyder Ali, and the latter scared of him. Second, Ali's son and successor, Tipu Sultan, had an independent grudge against the landlords who grew pepper. His incursions dispersed many of them and drove some towards Travancore state. Travancore, in turn, sought friendship with the British to deter Mysore.

Tellicherry was practically defenceless against Mysore and the coastal fleet Hyder Ali had created. Its closest ally, Bombay, had its worries with the Marathas and could not help when war broke out between Hyder Ali and the British in 1780. Ali's stranglehold on overland routes made it impossible for Tellicherry to avoid negotiating from a position of weakness. The British commanders saw some success when the battles were closer to the coast, but their attempts to capture the crucial overland route connecting the east and the west coasts at Palghat failed with serious loss of ammunition and lives.

And yet, shortly after this episode, the political equation began to change. It changed partly because of a new alliance against Mysore but also because of the resettlement of heads of prominent Indian merchant firms in Tellicherry, where they thought they were less exposed to potential extortion by the agents of the Mysore state. '[T]he leading merchants of Malabar (Chavacara Musa, Baile Babajee, Bedocandy Amed, and Banabeli Abdullah) fled to Tellicherry, which they regarded as the "oasis of peace and security and good government".'[80] Merchants were increasingly divided into factions allied with the British or the anti-British camps. The British camp was bigger. Tellicherry needed to keep the merchants happy because the Mysorean coastal fleet, on several occasions, tried to stop the rice supply from Konkan to the British factories.

Controlling overland routes was critical for all parties engaged in war. Mysore's power over the western coast rested on controlling two roads that cut through the Western Ghats. One of these crossed the mountain in a thinly populated part of it. This was vital for the movements of soldiers but not a critical trade route. The other route was different. Hyder Ali built one of his strongest forts in Palghat. The town flourished from the 1760s as a trading hub. It was significant in providing a link between Malabar and Coromandel coasts and access to other towns in the region, chiefly Dindigul and Coimbatore. 'Tipu's experience of the Second Anglo-Mysore War', said Mohibbul Hasan Khan, 'had taught him that, in case of another conflict with the English, Palghat

---

[80] Bonaventure Swai, 'East India Company and Moplah Merchants of Tellicherry: 1694–1800', *Social Scientist*, 8(1), 1979, 58–70. M. Arun Thomas and Asokan Mundon, 'Robert Adams: The Real Founder of English East India Company's Supremacy in Malabar', *IOSR Journal of Humanities and Social Science*, 20(5), 2015, 19–26.

would be again one of the first objects of their attack because, apart from other advantages, it offered them the only means of establishing an easy and practical communication between the Malabar and Coromandel coasts'.[81]

Before the advent of Mysore, three kings ruled the politics of Malabar: the Nair king of Palghat, the zamorin of Calicut, and the king of Cochin. The Dutch Company, closest ally of the Cochin Rajah, was an insignificant military force. Hyder Ali captured the vital space, Palghat, in the 1760s, leading two of these threatened kings to ask for British help. The British understood well enough how holding Palghat would change the balance. Between 1768 and 1790, the fort was occupied by Mysore or by the British. From 1783 onwards, British military units in South India would try again to capture the Palghat Pass and the fertile valley around it. Effectively, from 1783, Mysore's hold on the fort ended, and Palghat increasingly became the base of the military operations that eventually delivered the British victory in the fourth Anglo-Mysore war.

In sources on the final conflict, merchants remain obscure players. But their role cannot be overlooked. Palghat was not just a fort. It was a grain market and had some of the most fertile rice lands of South India. As a trading hub, which Hyder Ali had done much to develop, Palghat had no problem sustaining itself. For the British, it had all the promises of a successful bazaar strategy. Located close to the northern mountain pass, a British ally, the king of Coorg, gathered a large stock of rice, which sustained the army from Bombay and marched uphill towards the borders of Mysore. More rice came from the grain merchants of Malabar.[82]

Let us take a pause and return to the central theme of Section 2 before concluding this section. Did famines somehow disappear from India in the eighteenth century, or did these disasters not matter anymore?

Famines Still Mattered

Famines reappeared throughout the eighteenth century, most intensely in Bengal in 1770 and northern India in 1783. A systematic register of famines did not exist before 1770, nor was there an annual revenue dataset for any of the successor states to suggest when the states faced an external crisis like famine and war. The most systematic data came from the company's records or the works it sponsored. They wanted to know whether disasters affected state capacity and how badly they did, for some of these accounts touched on that

---

[81] Mohibbul Hasan Khan, *History of Tipu Sultan*, Calcutta and Dacca: The Bibliophile, 1951, 157.

[82] House of Lords, *Copies and Extracts of such Parts of the Correspondence between the Governor General, and the Governments of India respectively, with the Court of Directors, and the Secret Committee thereof, as relate to Hostilities with the late Tippoo Sultan*, 1799, 63.

aspect. The question that interests the Element is: when famines affected state capacity, which state's capacity was affected more?

The *Seir-ul-Mutakharin* of Ghulam Husain Tabatabai, prepared in the 1770s in Bengal, was a Persian political history of India until the rise of the British, written for the benefit of British officers. The book mentions famine often in relation to blockades and siege warfare. A famine broke out in western Bengal around 1746 after the Maratha invasion. Food was used as a weapon of war in the third battle of Panipat, 1761, that virtually ended Maratha ambition to rule northern India. Panipat was a conventional war between two large armies, but during the long prelude to the battle, deliberately prolonged by the Afghan warlord Ahmed Shah Abdali, the contest for food became intense. The Afghan-led coalition, 'eternally roaming round the Marhatta intrenchment, did not suffer a corn of grain or a blade of grass to find its way thither; insomuch that nothing being brought to the Marhatta camp', to show them 'what it was that the world called distress and famine'.[83]

The Seir offers probably the first partially bureaucratic narrative of a famine. This was the 1769–70 Bengal famine. The famine started with two consecutive failures of the rains, followed by floods and epidemics. The East India Company shared the civil administration with the Nawab of Bengal, and neither party trusted the other to share information on the extent of the crisis nor discussed how to mitigate it. The Seir indirectly confirmed that asymmetry of power and access to data weakened the relief effort. In the capital Murshidabad, the appointed 'overseers of the poor, proved so intent on their own interest, that so far from being able to procure plenty of grain, they were the foremost to use violent methods to engross it'.[84] The standard response of feudal states to famine was to commute taxes to the landlords, hoping they would use the money to provide relief. There was no way to know if they would do this. Carrying the suspicion that the landlords were loyal to the Nawab and hiding data, the Company refused to use this option. Anti-Company publicists in London, like Adam Smith and Edmund Burke, claimed that this inaction caused the famine. The truth is the disaster was too big to be dealt with by tax relief. The state earned too small a revenue to provide subsistence beyond a few days just by forgoing taxes.

Francis Buchanan Hamilton's 1807 journeys, again Company-sponsored, through the Mysore countryside reported evidence of abandoned villages and fields in the Tumkur area. He was told that these were the effects of a famine that had taken place in the wake of a conflict between the Maratha Peshwa and

---

[83] Hossein-Khan, *Seir Mutaqherin*, vol. 3 of 3, Calcutta: T.D. Chatterjee, 1902, 388.

[84] Hossein-Khan, *Seir Mutaqherin*, 58.

Hyder Ali of Mysore over control of the western hills and valleys.[85] The aftermath of the conflict lasted almost twenty years and drew in the Company forces. The third Anglo-Mysore war (1790–92) inflicted 'terrible misery' again: 'On the approach of the British army, the Sultan laid waste the whole country between this and the capital, . . . A large proportion . . . perished of hunger, or of the diseases following too scanty a diet.'[86]

The last great famine in northern India was the Chalisa of 1783. Its epicentre was probably Rohilkhand (see Map 1). The Company did not rule the region, but it did have a deep interest in it because, as an ally of the Awadh state, it had fought a war there. Besides, the Rohilla state, formed of decommissioned mercenaries of the Afghan army, was regarded with some anxiety by the Company. The famine is now attributed to an ENSO phenomenon that disrupted the monsoon cycle. Too little is known about how it developed and ended.

How did these disasters affect business and power, especially on the seaboard? Except for the Bengal famine of 1770, the other episodes almost certainly helped rather than adversely affected the East India Company's power. It did most directly during the Maratha raids of Bengal, pushing many wealthy Bengalis towards Calcutta. The Bengal famine did not change that balance. It did not because the British Indian state did not do much anyway and because there was no report that Calcutta, where its power was still concentrated, was affected. Calcutta was surrounded by a highly fertile delta land. There was neither dearth nor death there. The famine and mass deaths were most intense in the semi-arid western districts several hundred miles north of the city. The famine exposed the rift between the state's federal and local branches but had no serious effect on political power.

In the nineteenth century, the British ruled over half of India. Famines and droughts were more carefully registered. These episodes questioned policy or its absence. They did not affect politics because the state was no longer a work in progress. With that digression over, let us return to the core theme of Section 3, forging connections.

Conclusion

The key takeaway from this complex history is that, whereas a seaboard site might provide a benign environment for merchants, not all sites would give them good access to inland resources. Using those that did would entail

---

[85] Francis Buchanan, *A Journey from Madras through The Countries of Mysore, Canara, and Malabar*, London: T. Cadell and W. Davies, 1807, 6.
[86] Ibid., 63.

collaboration with local capitalists. These connections were critical in the beginning of the British Empire in India.

For some time, the French Company, Britain's principal enemy in India, worked similarly. They built military capability using connections made and knowledge gathered through trade. The French were more militaristic and some way ahead of the British Company around 1750. 'The raising of actual native regiments was first undertaken by the French, and it was due to the coming struggle for mastery in Southern India that we owe the first conception of a regular native army.' The French army was more disciplined and homogenous.[87]

But one factor differentiated the two forces. The British were strikingly more successful in drawing indigenous capital and skills away into their realm. They could keep the financial burden of running Bombay, Madras, and Calcutta manageable via what I called the bazaar strategy. The strategy worked because their seaboard situation enabled transactions in a variety of goods inside these towns. These places grew as a result. That economy allowed the British to raise an infantry army of Indian soldiers, a far more formidable force than the French counterpart.

Why were some of these places attractive to indigenous capital and skill? That topic occupies the next section.

4 Creating Cities in the Nineteenth Century

In the final part of the narrative, I will show how Indo-European trade laid the foundation for the emergence of port cities. That process of urban growth was not initially dependent on foreign investment but on the relocation of indigenous capital from the inland to the coastland (Figure 5). From the end of the eighteenth century, in some cases earlier, that process was dependent on and encouraged the migration of Indigenous capital and a great variety of skilled labour into these places. These mutually reinforcing processes of concentration of capital and diversification of skills made an agglomeration possible. By that term, I mean the ability to grow in population and livelihoods to generate further growth in population and livelihoods.

The fall of the Mughal Empire and the ensuing disturbances to trade in the core imperial zone drove trading and banking firms to relocate to the capitals of the successor states in central, southern, and eastern India. It was no longer possible for merchants who had financed river-borne trade in the Western Gangetic plains and transported grain across the western desert or the Himalayas to do so freely and safely. An earlier pattern of grain trade linked to revenue collection and despatch was consequently much smaller in scale. As the successor states

---

[87] MacMunn, *The Armies of India*, p. 4.

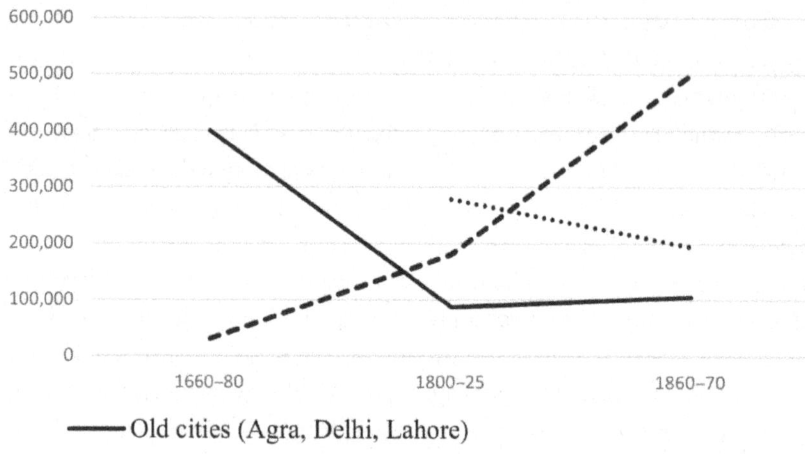

Figure 5 Average city population 1660–1870

Source: See Tirthankar Roy, *An Economic History of India 1707–1857*, London: Routledge, 2021.

engaged in wars in the latter half of the eighteenth century, some bankers and merchants retreated from this precarious setting to go to the Company towns.

Politics was a factor no doubt, but geography was another. Geography mattered in two ways. As Section 3 suggests, the seventeenth-century diversification was experimental in part and unsustainable, not least because defence required concentration of efforts. A reverse movement, from networks to nodes, was inevitable. Second, Bombay, Calcutta, and Madras were at the forefront of that movement. So far these places have not figured much in the narrative, because they were hardly different from the many smaller settlements the British Company was working with. But that was changing from the end of the eighteenth century.

For a long time after the towns were founded, and throughout the seventeenth century and much of the eighteenth, Bombay, Madras, and Calcutta represented distinct sorts of urbanism. The administration in Bombay, an accidental acquisition, was focused on town building. Madras, threatened by warlords and later the more formidable forces of Mysore and the French East India Company, was preoccupied with defence. Calcutta was more focused on trading. Until disputes with the local state changed the situation, Calcutta was a safer place and could concentrate on providing a space for merchants trading with the inland, with Asia, and Britain.

From the last quarter of the eighteenth century, their histories converged, as a more secure administration could concentrate on governance: law, police, security, and road and river communication. Ship repair was present in all. Bombay, with access to Malabar timber, became a major centre of the industry. In the nineteenth century, education and finance received much private, primarily indigenous, investment. The combination of these services set these cities apart from the state capitals in the interior. As they did, Indian capitalists moved into these cities to strengthen the financial markets and take over much of the coastal shipping, including the vast field of Arabian Sea trade. Bombay grew by drawing capital away from Surat, Madras from Coromandel, and Calcutta from western Bengal and the Company's capital from Balasore and other stations.

When that process reached maturity in the early nineteenth century with the expansion of opium, indigo, and cotton trades, many other settlements where Europeans once had traded declined. Seasonality was influential in driving this unequal urban process. Seasonality gave a transient character to the seaboard cities. S. Arasaratnam saw this precisely and factored it in an account of the decline of Coromandel ports: 'the ports did not develop as permanent settlements of merchants, they also did not attract artisans and thus did not grow as centres of handicraft production ... trade did not generate other economic activity in the ports, the capital that was attracted there for trade did not remain there' and so on.[88] Arasaratnam got it exactly right. This was the fate of most small settlements that never diversified away from the basic package – fort, warehouse, and ship repair. But a smaller set did break out of the constraints of monsoon seasonality.

Madras

The founding of Madraspatnam between 1632 and 1639 (when the first fort came up) was the most noteworthy event of the early seventeenth century. For some time, the English wanted to shift the centre of the Coast Agency from Masulipatam to a new settlement. Complaints about political interference and difficulty of navigation in the face of storms led to that decision. A southern base was preferred to develop commerce with Sind on the one hand and with the Malabar seaboard on the other. The chief (Nayak), who controlled the Madraspatnam area, welcomed the settlement and drew up an elaborate profit-sharing contract.

---

[88] Arasaratnam, 'Factors in the Rise, Growth and Decline of Coromandel Ports CIRCA 1650-1720', 19–30. Cited text on p. 29.

There were significant constraints to its growth in the seventeenth century. In the 1640s, investment decisions were constrained by the high cost of credit on the eastern coast and the high levels of debts the officers and merchants accumulated in Surat, Madras, and Bantam, under whose jurisdiction Madras came. The Company had no direct access or control inland. The rulers in neighbouring states negotiated with the Company for tribute, and when these negotiations failed, blockaded access to food coming from inland.[89] These attempts to blackmail were not sustainable. In 1657, during one such episode, the blockade failed because the sea was open to supply the inhabitants with food. The blockade caused merely inconvenience and stoppage of trade, which affected the revenue-paying capacity of the districts around. On another occasion, the Nawab 'soon after sued for pacification'.[90] These threats were an annoyance, nevertheless.

In the late seventeenth century, Madras acquired a special significance as the recipient of a great quantity of the silver peso the Manilla Galleons brought from the Americas to Asia. In India, silver coins were transformed into local currency and used as payment for goods. '[E]very year', the physician-traveller Niccolao Manucci wrote in 1686,

> there were earned in Madras five lakhs of gold pagodas (equal to about one million of patacas, more or less) and over ten lakhs of silver rupees (which amounts to five hundred thousand patacas). The whole of this money remained in the country, and in exchange for all this the English carried off to Europe no more than some cotton cloth.[91]

Five lakhs or half a million gold pagodas should amount to about £110 million today (for a coin of roughly 3.3 grams weight).

With the decline of the Galleon traffic in the late eighteenth century, and greater success of the British Company in selling iron and guns in India, access to silver was no more a strategic advantage. Madras rose to prominence in the first half of the eighteenth century mainly as a naval and military station. With rising Anglo-French conflict in India, the town was engaged in the Carnatic succession wars (1740–63) and was a target in the first Anglo-Mysore War (1767–69).

Once the French and Mysore threats receded, migration began in earnest. 'As political tensions in peninsular India increased during the [eighteenth] century', writes Susan Neild Basu, 'many important merchants, financiers, groups of skilled artisans, and others shifted their center of

---

[89] William Foster, *The English Factories in India 1655–1660*, Oxford: Clarendon Press, 1921, 182.

[90] Foster, *The English Factories in India 1655–1660*, 97.

[91] Niccolao Manucci, *Storia do Mogor*, 4 vols, London: John Murray, vol. 3, 390.

activity to Madras from waning coastal ports or unstable inland town'.[92] This migration remains under-researched in business history, as far as I am aware. However, it is a prominent subject for discussion among urban historians, for Madras around 1800 was constantly redrawing its boundary and extending the jurisdiction of justice and police to keep up with it. Telugu-speaking merchants who came from Coromandel shaped the demographic, religious, and commercial identity of these spaces that were incorporated into the town area. The present name for Madras, Chennai, originated in these spaces and was a tribute to their contribution to the making of the city.

Madras had a rapidly growing 'Black Town' (Figure 6). The term may mislead us into thinking there was an administrative policy of ethnic segregation. There was no such thing. Ethnicities lived apart because land transactions, tenancy, commercial law, and religious institutions were initially ethnicity-bound rather than governed by the town administration. By nineteenth century, these organic segregations were coming to an end.

Bombay

Bombay was a gift from the Portuguese Crown to the British Crown. 'His Majesty [whose possession Bombay was] intended to make the port of Bombaym the flourishing port in India.' But the king had no idea how to make that dream come true and handed over Bombay to the Company. The Company did not know either. The conditions were exceedingly grim and not because of political insecurity.[93] The latter did play a part. For decades, there was the fear of a contest for the Arabian Sea trade. 'We feared the Mogull might have sided with the Persian on behalf of his merchants . . . and thereupon [have] impeded the whole course of our business.'[94] These fears materialized towards the end of the century during a specific dispute.

On an everyday basis, Bombay's foul environment contributed to the problems. [V]ery few can live there', wrote an officer back to the head office shortly after the takeover, 'but such as are borne upon the place, the air and water are soe infectious'.[95] Bombay grew little food and had to depend on Gujarat for supplies. Its original inhabitants, a small settlement of Portuguese and Indo-Portuguese, complained of living in a permanent famine when the possession changed hands. There was no way to sell English goods or access big markets nearby. The Portuguese could be relied on to bring some food from Goa but

---

[92] Susan Neild Basu, 'Madras in 1800: Perceiving the City', *Studies in the History of Art*, 31, 1993, 221–240. Cited text on p. 222.

[93] Foster, *The English Factories in India 1668–69*, 8.   [94] Ibid., 31.   [95] Ibid., 27, 68.

Figure 6 Black Town in Madras, photographed by Frederick Fiebig
in the 1850s.

Source: Alamy, public domain image.

demanded a large commission 'being very disaffectionate and envious to our
nation'.[96]

Through most of the 1670s and the 1680s, Bombay's economy was periodic-
ally threatened by food shortages. The Modi, or house steward, became an
essential office under the town administration, the counterpart of the broker in
the trading stations. In the 1670s, a Parsi merchant, Cowas, held the office.
'Dearness of provisions' did not just restrict the size of a settlement but also
risked mutiny among soldiers. In Bombay in the 1670s, the persistent threat of
blockade by the Sidi navy became doubly awkward because some of the
soldiers mutinied, complaining of 'the dearness of provisions and the high
price of money . . . so that they could not live on their pay'.[97]

If food was a problem, water was a bigger problem. No wells on the island or
rivers and streams carried water in the dry months. Those who could pay for it
had water brought from Salsett (now suburban or Greater Mumbai). The
ordinary soldiers could not pay for it and suffered from 'flux and looseness'.

---

[96] Ibid., 50.
[97] Charles Fawcett, *The English Factories in India, vol. 1 (New Series) The Western Presidency
1670–1677*, Oxford: Clarendon Press, 1936, 92.

Acquiring territories like Salsett and Bassein was important in providing food supplies for people living in Bombay. 'The waters of Salcet in the Malabar coast where Bombay is located are wholesome and its soil fruitful, naturally abundant, and capable of great improvement.'[98] All port towns needed a hinterland, and Bombay needed it the most.

Unlike all other settlements in India, the Company documents concerning Bombay talk less about trade and more about urban administration and building the town's economy. From the start, Bombay relied on the textile trade much less than the other settlements or agencies. The town authority invited weavers to settle in and reduced duties on their raw materials. But not much export trade followed. Instead, the town tried to become a shipping hub and build its economy. To do this, the authorities reduced customs (initially auctioning the customs collection to reduce expenditure), encouraged local manufacturing, and encouraged ship repair and timber trade. It started a mint suitable for producing copper coins. Governor Gerald Aungier wanted more public buildings in the town.

Politics frustrated these efforts. A conflict had broken out in the 1670s between the Sidi naval commanders with ties to the Mughals and the Marathas trying to subdue them. The appearance of ships and soldiers within a few miles of the town caused food inflation in Bombay. The British attempted to maintain neutrality. Their investments in Surat-based trade made them afraid of the Mughals, and their reliance on Maratha territories for food supplies worried them about upsetting the Marathas. In the 1680s, they tried to defeat the Sidis, but failed. Further south, the 'malevolent Portuguese' tried to disrupt supplies, though considerable private trade between Portuguese merchants and Bombay merchants continued. Similarly, to the north, the Mughal representatives in Broach and Surat were wary of the export of food that the Marathas might capture.

The persistent problem with food prices led the town administration to introduce some market regulations. A similar set of controls came up in the matter of commissions the bankers charged on the exchange of currencies. These interventions were not one-sided but based on public meetings between the administrators and the indigenous bankers and merchants, in which deals were negotiated and rates were reduced against privileges. In this way, the indigenous capitalists and the Company administration shared a common negotiating platform for which no exact parallel existed in Madras or Calcutta.

The Company sometimes had to go out of its way to maintain this obligation. One incident occurred in 1675. Shivaji had bought provisions from

---

[98] Anon., *An Historical Account of the Settlement and Possession of Bombay by the East India Company*, London: W. Richardson, 1781.

merchants connected to Bombay by having a party in Golconda issue a bill. This person subsequently went missing. The Bombay governor took up the case on behalf of the merchants and negotiated with Shivaji's ministers, who did not deny the claim but wanted to honour it with some goods seized in battle and valued well above fair price. A year later, another awkwardness developed. A group of dancing girls left the Maratha territory and disappeared in Bombay. Shivaji's minister reminded Aungier that since the former was obliged to hand over fugitives from Bombay, the latter should do the same thing: find these girls, and return them. The incident made Aungier think that a permanent diplomatic mission at the Maratha court might be a good idea, though nothing came of it.[99]

The eighteenth century saw these hostilities recede. Bombay was exposed to a potential attack by the Maratha forces, but the political administration was keen to keep relations with the Marathas friendly, no less because the interior access through the mountains was crucial for food supplies, and the Maratha forces controlled these routes. The Marathas, in turn, were increasingly too preoccupied with inland contests to break the relationship. Bombay's strengths consisted of access to the Arabian Sea trade with Africa and West Asia and access to the Deccan Plateau via a gap through the mountains that the Company hoped to keep safe by maintaining good relations with the Peshwas. Section 3 also showed how the Maratha factor induced Bombay's administration and merchants to renegotiate ties with merchants inland and food and timber suppliers in coastal trades.

A trader headquartered in a port city could access many opportunities in the early nineteenth century. The two rising trade commodities of the late eighteenth century were opium and cotton. Marwari merchants established a connection between Bombay and central India through their involvement in opium in the interior. Cotton exports were handled by Gujarati and Parsi merchants who were either based in Bombay or had a substantial presence there. Beginning around the end of the eighteenth century, Bombay Port's cotton export to China grew, which fostered the migration of Parsi, Bhatia, and Marwari commercial families to the city. They carried with them overland and Asian trading experience. After the British defeated the Marathas in 1818, a sizeable area of the cotton-growing region was directly connected to the city and the export market.

By contrast with Bengal (see the discussion on Calcutta below), merchant migration on the western and eastern littoral in the late eighteenth century were a lot more protracted and voluntary. In a received view, Surat declined because

---

[99] Fawcett, *The English Factories in India, vol. 1 (New Series)*, 148.

of its internal politics and the fall of some of the great family business firms there, encouraging a flight of capital towards Bombay. This view stands much revised.[100] The decline of Surat was partly the East India Company's own making; its tariff policy affected big groups engaged in Surat-West-Asia traffic. The flight of capital, possibly exaggerated, was not one-directional, and benefited small seaports in peninsular Gujarat operating under the active encouragement of a string of coastal states.[101] There may have been a relative decline still, in the sense that without Bombay being there, a great deal of the money and services tied up with overland and West Asia trade in Gujarat might have gone to Surat. It now went to Bombay. With the Parsis, there was a clearer and direct impulse to congregate in Bombay.

What the Telugu merchants represented in Madras, the Parsis did on the western littoral. A few Parsis from western India served as the Company's brokers. Many more were well-known as independent shipwrights and merchants by 1820. They started as carpenters, moved into shipbuilding and repair in Surat and Bombay around the close of the 1700s, and eventually became merchants. These talents were acquired through a well-designed artisanal apprenticeship system that guaranteed the master-builder status was passed down through the family. They were among the first Indian merchants and seafarers to study shipbuilding in England. This exposure was necessary when the 1840s saw the switch from sail to steam. The alteration was executed relatively smoothly by the Parsi master-builders.

Groups of Parsis were recognized as prospective participants in the developing Indo-China commerce due to their well-established status as shipwrights and their familiarity with the timber markets. When the Company's India monopoly ended in 1813, and it sold some of its ships at a discount, the Parsi shippers purchased several of the ships. They refurbished them for coastal or China traffic when the business started withdrawing from the Indian trade (after 1813) and the China trade (the charter terminated in 1833). These ships were active during the Wars with Burma (1824) and China (1839). Large amounts of tea transported from China over the Atlantic were paid for with the earnings from the sale of Indian opium, which had already become the country's principal export to China. The Parsi shippers were important in the Calcutta-Canton

---

[100] The most comprehensive discussion of Surat's history through the late eighteenth-century transition, and the related historiographical debates, can be found in Ghulam A. Nadri, *Eighteenth-Century Gujarat: The Dynamics of its Political Economy, 1750–1800*, Leiden and Boston: Brill, 2009.

[101] Ghulam A. Nadri, 'Exploring the Gulf of Kachh: Regional Economy and Trade in the Eighteenth Century', *Journal of the Economic and Social History of the Orient*, 51(3), 2008, 460–486.

and Bombay-Canton cargo movement. In West Asia and East Africa, Parsi presence increased at the same time.

Calcutta

Although Bengal was, in many ways, rich in resources, including food, water, and trading goods, Calcutta was not a great choice for building a settlement. The territory that made up Calcutta in its early days consisted of wetlands, marshes, and land submerged seasonally from overflowing rivers and monsoon rains. Lower Bengal Delta's numerous waterways made moving cargo cheap if season-bound. These channels were susceptible to silt deposits that made navigation even when the monsoons had passed a challenging proposition. Like Bombay, the area was disease-prone. Building a city in this environment required interventions in law, medicine, and infrastructure, which took off in the nineteenth century, not before.[102] The very low rent with which the Company could lease the land reflected the value attached to it by the local landlords. So, what drove this choice?

Job Charnock, the Company officer who ran into trouble with the provincial government and tried to escape an army by navigating down the Hooghly River, stopped on this bank probably by accident. He must have sensed that from a safety point of view, this was a good choice for a settlement, as it was surrounded by swamps and rivers on three sides. This little area was an ungoverned space because of its low value and the natural defences. That advantage played a large role in the town's growth in the mid eighteenth century.

During 1740–52, Maratha light cavalry regiments stationed in central India repeatedly raided Bengal and conquered the southwest regions. There were no state-led and coordinated warfare. Generals and mercenaries commanded them. The purpose of the raids was to force the Nawab of Bengal to share the province's revenue and, if that failed, to extract money from people living in the western and southwestern areas of Bengal, where the cavalry invaded the country. During retreats, the soldiers made sure the western region would lose its ability to pay taxes for one season. Food and fodder became scarce, some of it was burnt, the markets were burnt down, the chief banker 'Jugget Seat's factory, and other capital houses' were plundered in Murshidabad.[103] The Nawab lost both money and the ability to defend, and when treaties were signed, was forced to squeeze the taxpayers hard. The Company, too, contributed to the defence. In

---

[102] Debjani Bhattacharyya, *Empire and Ecology in the Bengal Delta: The Making of Calcutta*, New York: Cambridge University Press, 2018.

[103] For citations on this subject, Salimullah, *Tarikh I Bangal*, volume 2 of 2, trans. Francis Gladwin, Calcutta: J. W. Fischer of Stuart and Cooper, 1785, 194–197.

1752, when the raids stopped with the assassination of a general (Mir Habib) on the Maratha side, the state's fiscal and political affairs were in ruins, a confusion that the Company officers who defeated the Nawab in 1757 benefited from.

The Maratha episode was vital to Calcutta's rise. The Maratha army did not attempt to embargo or halt trade from Calcutta, except for 1748. The potential cost of an attack on Calcutta almost certainly outweighed the benefits given the natural defences of the place. For the same reason, Calcutta became a destination for wealthy refugees. Baneshwar Bidyalankar, a contemporary writer, gave a graphic account of wealthy merchants and Brahmins leaving their homes, carrying whatever capital or tools of the trade they thought were most helpful to start a new life.[104] As 'the country, from Akbarnagar to Midnapoor, and Jaleshwar, was over-run with the invaders; who committed unparallelled acts of cruelty and extortion', said another chronicler Salimullah, 'many of the principal people fled to the eastern end of the Ganges, and settled in those provinces, with their families'.[105] For most, the destination was Calcutta.

Landlords had no option but to stay and negotiate. Much of the western Bengal was left under Mir Habib, who negotiated revenue payments with prominent landlords. Most refugees belonged to two professional classes – merchants and service providers – possessing portable capital and skills. Ramdulal Sarkar, the great shipping magnate and the principal associate of the American merchants in late eighteenth-century Calcutta, was born on the roads when his parents fled from home. Two Bengali merchants, Shobharam Basak and Baishnabcharan Seth, were the chief financiers of the defences of Calcutta. Basak came from a family that had been producing and trading silk and cotton textiles for generations. His father Ganganarayan was a partner and agent of the Dutch East India Company. Shobharam was an agent for the British Company and was close to the French of Chandannagar. Like many textile trading families of sixteenth-century Bengal, the family firm had several bases, including Saptagram, the most important river port before the seventeenth century, Midnapur, and Murshidabad, the capital of Bengal. In the 1740s, all three places were targets of attack when Shobharam shifted operations to Calcutta. Saptagram was also one of the bases of Bengal's most prominent business caste, the Subarnabaniks. Community lore says that in the 1740s, principal Subarnabanik families and their firms left their bases in western Bengal to relocate closer to the river. Some came to Calcutta. Others moved to towns under French and Dutch control (see Figure 7).[106]

---

[104] Haraprasad Shastri, 'Baneshwar Bidyalankar', *Sahitya-Parishat-Patrika* [Bengali] 38, 1938, 135–144.

[105] Salimullah, *Tarikh-i-Bangla*, 196–197.

[106] Shibchandra Shil, *Gaure Suarnabanik* [Bengali, Subarnabaniks in Gaur], Chunchura: Author, 1910, 49.

Figure 7 House of a wealthy Indian on the banks of the Hooghly, photographed by Frederick Fiebig in the 1850s. Fiebig travelled in South Asia, and like his contemporary Felice Beato, photographed subjects and landscapes that embodied the history of the region. The East India Company purchased a part of his collection.

Source: Alamy, public domain image.

Merchant migration to Bengal had an older history. Following the Mughal conquest of Bengal in 1595, Punjabi Khatri people migrated to eastern India. They resettled as merchants, tax farmers, landholders, court officers, and military officers. One of the main agents of the East India Company in Bengal during the 1750s was the Khatri merchant Amirchand, who played a prominent part in the passage of state power from the Nawab to the Company's hands.

C. A. Bayly has shown that town merchants in North India adapted well to the political transition after the British takeover. They maintained continuity in their way of life and commercial dealings through their associations, corporations, and temples.[107] British expansion in the region did not affect their economic significance or social cohesiveness. Indeed, as the Mughal imperial power receded but British colonial power spread, market integration spanning the Indo-Gangetic Basin gave merchants and bankers access to a broader area,

---

[107] Bayly, *Rulers, Townsmen and Bazaars* .

including the fertile Bengal Delta, and a wider range of produce. Colonialism reduced their transaction costs and offered new investment opportunities.

If the Khatris came as Mughal allies, migrating Marwari merchants and banking houses to Calcutta and middle-Bengal towns was more of a business venture. The most well-known of these firms started in Rajputana, where they could take advantage of financial opportunities provided by the East-West trade routes as well as legal autonomy and protection granted by the princely states. Throughout the eighteenth century, the Rajput territories endured crippling succession disputes, frequent attacks by central Indian Maratha forces, and a state of disorder in the trade routes they were supposed to protect. Some then moved from this base to Hyderabad and Indore in the eighteenth century. However, in about 1800, these firms preferred British possessions, suggesting that either the implicit guarantee of stability was insufficient or that business prospects had dried up.

The 1740s exodus consolidated the Company's plan to set up revenue-generating markets. From the early 1700s, the Company was resolved to make Calcutta pay for itself. The marketplaces or bazaars that the new administration established served as the hub of this industry. The markets were used to tax almost everything that was sold there. Given the variety of local resources and artisanal services, the list of taxed goods was long and diverse. Marriages and contracts incurred licence fees. In a study attempting to uncover a method in the 'confused chaos' (William McKintosh's words) that was Calcutta during the first forty years, Farhat Hasan discovers it in the bazaar, where taxes collected rose from nine to 28 per cent of annual revenue between 1713 and 1743.[108] Since the rent of the place did not change, the Company's payment for it dropped to an insignificant proportion. In the second half of the eighteenth century, the bazaar strategy was an integral part of urban governance.[109]

Capital Draws in Capital

With the concentration of trade and merchant migration, these cities developed an environment that was different from that in the inland towns, the key ingredients of which were commercial law, a deep financial market, and opportunities to access higher education, enabling graduates of the new system to join trade, finance, and modern business.

---

[108] Farhat Hasan, 'Indigenous Cooperation and the Birth of a Colonial City: Calcutta, c. 1698–1750', *Modern Asian Studies*, 26(1), 1992, 65–82.

[109] A new scholarship explores this dimension of the Company's spatial policy. See Kaustubh Mani Sengupta, 'Bazaars, Landlords, and the Company Government in Late Eighteenth-Century Calcutta', *Indian Economic and Social History Review*, 52(2), 2015, 121–146; and Anirban Karak, 'The Politics of Commerce in Eighteenth-Century Bengal: A Reappraisal', *Indian Economic and Social History Review*, 61(1), 2024, 33-66.

Employees inside the factories carried on a private credit business with people outside. It was a high-return-high-risk enterprise. Little is known about how it was conducted and what happened when there was default. On one occasion in 1668, a Balasore employee, Thomas Stiles, petitioned the town's governor to recover a debt. Facing an enquiry back at the factory, he revealed that such petitions were not uncommon, and the governor usually intervened on behalf of the creditor, taking a 30 per cent cut on the money recovered.[110]

Fifty years later, the business of intercontinental trade and Indian financial markets were much more closely integrated. Indian bankers were a source of support for both the Company and private traders. Two important services they provided were transferring money between Indian districts and converting Spanish money into Indian currency. With coin valuation in a world where nearly all valuable coins were composed of gold and silver alloys, reputation was important. As a result, not many people were involved in this industry. Remittance was another important service. The Company transferred money between branches using bankers' drafts drawn on Indian banking houses in the eighteenth century. Once more, reputation was critical. Western India had a comparatively more significant development of these services than Eastern India. Not surprisingly, most if not all, of the corporate banks in British India formed in these three cities.

A second attraction of these cities was education. Business communities invested significantly in the education of their children. British artisans tutored Indians in the cities. David Hare, the watchmaker of Calcutta, did much more and helped set up several schools and a college. Missions engaged in education and inspired Indians to set up schools or teach. One of the earliest examples in Bombay, a school was established by the Parsi community for their children to learn English.[111] In 1838, the great shipwright of Surat, Nowrojee Jamsetji, sent his son and nephew to England to learn the craft of building steamships. The master-builders recorded their impression of British society in a note. After giving an account of the education of female children in a middle-class English family, they wrote, we have thus given the particulars of the acquirements and education of young females in England, to induce mothers in India ... to establish some such system to educate their children. Why should they not have boarding schools conducted as the English ones, always having female teachers therein instead of males ... if they could but know the host of

---

[110] Foster, *The English Factories in India 1668–69*, 165.

[111] Anon., *An Historical Account of the Settlement and Possession of Bombay by the East India Company*.

amusements and recreations that by education are afforded to females.[112] These words expressed a sentiment widely shared among Indian business communities working in the three port towns, but it was conspicuously absent in the inland towns.

Curiously enough, the Company government was far more conservative. From the late eighteenth century, the British administrators wanted to preserve an Indian mode of education, not least because they wanted to settle civil law cases with reference to Indian indigenous codes rather than European ones. This conservationist approach had few takers among Indian people in the three cities. Wealthy Indian merchants did not care much for Sanskrit poetry but wanted English education and scientific and technical education in Calcutta and Bombay. Major institutions of the early nineteenth century – the Elphinstone College in Bombay (c. 1840), Calcutta Medical College, the Grant Medical College in Bombay, the Hindu College in Calcutta, and scholarships at the University of Bombay – were funded by Indian business profits. When, in 1835, the law adviser to the Company state, T. B. Macaulay, issued a statement that state education should prioritize scientific Westernized curricula rather than follow Indian classics, he was merely endorsing an action plan the Indian business communities had been following for decades.

There was more than teaching skills behind the impetus. There was a new valuation of knowledge. Producers of goods and services were using a more diverse range of tools and processes than before. The Company state and many Indian subjects lived in the shadow of an ongoing scientific-technological revolution. Members of both sets believed that transmitting useful knowledge from Britain to India would be a good thing. That idea was not a top-down imposition. Indians understood this point better than the British administrator. They hired skilled personnel from abroad, sponsored higher and technical education, and set up colleges and schools to impart Western scientific knowledge, where many instructors came from abroad (see also Figure 8).

There was also a distinct aspect to the mode of governance of these towns.

Law

The port city legal system was a hybrid initially, separate codes if not separate courts for Europeans and non-Europeans. But this separation was an unstable one, and in commercial disputes, unsustainable. By the nineteenth century, there

---

[112] Anon., 'Journal of a Residence in Great Britain, by Jehungeer Nowrajee and Hirjeebhoy Merwanjee, of Bombay, Naval Architects. London. 1841', *Calcutta Review*, 4, 1845, Miscellaneous Notices, i–xii.

Figure 8 Chandannagar Strand. As the empire consolidated, the character of the trading towns changed, from commercial-naval bases to places where education, entertainment, and good living came together. The still beautiful promenade along the river in this former French colony was a symbol of good life.

Source: Author.

was substantial convergence in contract cases. An 1872 Act formalized that convergence by drawing entirely on Western codes.

There were differences between the Mughal system of law and justice in North India and the British colonial one in the ports. First, the latter was secular rather than religious in origin, and in practice available to non-Europeans. Being English in source, it allowed a much larger space for contracts, debt recovery, and provisions related to property, especially the property of the expatriates, whereas both Hindu and Muslim laws were preoccupied with the personal and the virtuous. A noticeable difference, for example, was in respect of maritime laws. The innovations in this regard were extended to new institutions such as the Small Causes Courts and Insolvent Courts, both designed to deal with cases of debt and commercial contracts.

Second, whereas the Mughal system of justice created an identity between state-defined laws and state-backed courts in civil matters, in effect leaving most commercial disputes to be settled by community norms and informal mechanisms, the port cities departed from the practice. There was increasingly one hierarchical court system to settle all disputes. The new courts became sites where both new and old laws could be practiced. The Mughal system of justice recognized two broad classes of people: Muslims and others. The British system likewise distinguished between the expatriates and others, leaving the latter to enjoy the protection of their respective customs while taking over the task of coding, defining, and implementing customs using paid experts. But the others did not just consist of Hindus and Muslims, also Sikhs, Christians, Portuguese, Parsis, Armenians, Buddhists, and hundreds of others besides. The Muslims and Hindus themselves were not homogenous communities, and the divisions within them were reflected in a highly diverse and often contradictory jurisprudence. The new courts grappled with this diversity, and in effect, narrowed the space where religious law still ruled.

More than politics or ideology, economics decided this system's broad contours of evolution. Rather than personal life, honour, or privileges, property rights were increasingly debated in the courts. Between 1793 and 1830, private property rights in land had become codified as a by-product of reforms in the land taxation system. An alienable property right in land demanded well-defined laws of succession and inheritance. Customary laws always gave much importance to inheritance, succession, and gifts, both as integral parts of the continuity of lineages and as a means to ensure security of property.

Conclusion

The key message from the section is that the port cities represented an emergent and broadly stable partnership between Indian capital and British power based on a perception of mutual advantages. All states may need such a partnership. In the eighteenth century, any such collaboration in the interior of India was either crumbling or severely tested by conflicts. In the coastlands, it was more stable. Politics alone would not explain that stability. A benign geography played its part.

Between 1750 and 1850, it would be impossible to imagine an agglomeration of the nature described in this section happening in an interior city, which was still dependent on the monsoon seasonality, the collection of revenue from land, the risks that came with it, religious law and the most basic education sponsored by communities, and access to which was restricted. Under the right conditions, the seaboard cities could grow faster because they could diversify livelihoods faster and were less susceptible to seasonality. Their ability to link land and sea, connections with overland trade, political security, the attraction of a benign environment, and the service economy of the cities, combined to sustain the agglomeration process. A network of seaside trading settlements gave way to concentration into nodes – both on the western coast and east.

A significant spill-over of the agglomeration process was industrialization. As Britain saw the beginning of industrialization, a convergence began between British industrialization and Indian capability based in the three port towns. Aided by the integration of regions through imperialism and, later, the railways, indigenous private capital based in the port cities started taking firmer control over the agricultural commodity trade inland on a scale unprecedented in the region. With control over the cotton trade, it was feasible to reinvest trading profits in textile mills, giving rise to the world's fourth-largest textile mill complexes in the late nineteenth century. In other raw materials too (sugarcane, wheat, oilseeds, jute), Indians controlled the trade, though the industries that used these materials, if they produced for export (as jute), received a great deal of British investment. By contrast with this urban and partly coastal industrialization, the interior remained largely artisanal until the twentieth century.

When India gained independence in 1947, its port towns housed a well-functioning legal system, and some of the best educational institutions, medical facilities, banks, insurance providers, and learned institutions outside the West. Indian industrialists and merchants had contributed significantly to the creation of that infrastructure. We need to look no further than this vibrant service economy of the three port cities to explain their attraction for migrants, especially middle-class migrants. Migrants from abroad and from India built the service economy, and in turn, migrants drew in other migrants. An open market in services, the ability of employers to hire with minimum fuss the right sorts of skilled people (that included many Europeans) was the key. This trade in services significantly contributed to business growth and the attraction of the cities in the nineteenth century.

5 Beyond India

I will not claim in this section that the narrative of the origin of empires offered in Sections 2–4 works for the whole world. The emergence of European rule in Asia and Africa was far too complex to be reduced to one narrative valid from the Caribbean to the Pacific. In the nineteenth century, colonial powers decided to possess territories in response to their rivals' policies. Territorial claims came before governance began. The narrative of origin would not work there.

However, the intuition that *place matters* remains valid, if not in explaining the pathway, then in explaining the diverse pattern of colonial rule and its many-sided legacies. How does it matter? Almost everywhere, seaboard sites were critical. These sites were trading places. In a tropical setting, a seaboard site for trade had better chances to procure food, water, or the resources needed to maintain a commercial and military infrastructure than an inland one. When the site had a long history of commodity trade, indigenous and European merchants shared the space. An intercontinental and cosmopolitan trading history encouraged the concentration of power to protect trade.

Place mattered, too, because not all seaboard sites were similar. Some had fertile agricultural land surrounding them, some were islands and transit ports, and some did not have much of an agricultural hinterland to subsist on. It is impossible to generalize about how these variations shaped imperial power. However, one limited hypothesis should hold: colonial power depended on urban spaces, and the capacity of urban space to sustain population growth and attract wealth depended on its connections with other spaces. These connections were partly geographically mediated. Land and sea integration was geographically mediated, especially in tropical areas where arid climatic conditions began within a few hundred miles of the coast, sometimes much closer. However militarily powerful and however much they received the backing of the parent state, if the inland offered a harsh environment, colonial power stepped back and compromised, producing a limited form of rule.

In this section, I will demonstrate the hypothesis – that a harsh environment imposed limits upon state power and urbanism – with one example: Northeast Africa. Like South Asia, this region (mainly the Horn of Africa) was located within a few hundred miles of the Tropic of Cancer and experienced extreme aridity. The seaboard to the south of the Horn fell in the pathway of the Southwest Monsoon of the Northern Hemisphere. Compared with South Asia, the monsoon was weak. The rest of the region received a monsoon that was even weaker and uncertain. Unlike South Asia, the inland offered little serious incentive to the seaboard merchants. While commercialization was present on the coast from centuries before Italian-French-British colonization, the main livelihood of the inland was animal herding, with caravans linking the sea with more benign environments beyond the arid tracts.

There were broad similarities in the commercialization trajectory between South Asia and Northeast Africa, such as the growth of trade in inland goods, European settlement and control, collaboration with indigenous merchants, and urban growth. And yet, unlike South Asia, the colonial experience was short-lived. It did not deeply impact material life, and the capacity and the intent to secure power inland seemed missing. The states that emerged looked nothing like British India. Colonialism was a distant, hands-off mode of power, governing territories with a light touch. Commerce and urbanism played minor parts in that kind of colonialism. Again, confirming the intuition that places matter, the highlands were exceptions to the harsh ecology. These highlands had not been too agricultural or commercial before the transition to European rule but emerged as military-political centres during it, among other reasons, because the Europeans wanted to escape the heat of the plains.

Most of this section is about the Horn. As we move southward from the Horn, the monsoon becomes stronger and the arid inland narrower. Here, a slightly different trajectory of colonialism emerged, which I show in a later section.

Trade, Colonialism, and Urban Spaces: Northeast Africa

Northeast Africa consists of countries in the Horn of Africa (Somalia, Somaliland, Eritrea, Djibouti, Puntland, and the Ethiopian plains). This area is 400–700 miles south of the Tropic of Cancer. Summer temperatures rise to extreme levels. Whereas a monsoon does occur, its strength is significantly weaker than in South Asia. Average summer temperatures are similar. But the average annual precipitation in the Horn is about a third to a quarter of that in South Asia. Although both India and Somalia receive the Southwest monsoon of the Northern Hemisphere, the rainiest areas of India get ten times more rain (2818 mm in Assam) than Somalia (on average 280 mm). Within the Horn, the southern seaboard has more rainfall and river water. The two main rivers (Juba and Shabelle) originate in the Ethiopian mountains. Still, because of the monsoonal difference, river water flow is, on average, much lower than that of South Asian and West African rivers and drops sharply in the dry months (May–September, December–March). Not surprisingly, arable land is confined to the river valleys and formed about 10 per cent of the area in Somalia (around 1960). In the remaining area, animal husbandry was the dominant livelihood, even the only form of livelihood. The low plateau inland, which merges into Ethiopia's mountains, is cooler but drier.

The Horn represents a puzzle to the historian. 'When we think of the formation of the nation/state in Sub-Saharan African history', writes Irma Taddia, historian of Eritrea, 'we tend to isolate the Horn of Africa from other African ex-colonial societies and to analyze it as a peculiar phenomenon'.[113] This view is influenced by the unique characteristics of the imperial influence under mainly Italian rule and, consequently, postcolonial nationalism, which was not like what the French and British colonies went through. I will suggest in the section that the unique characteristics of the Horn of Africa and colonialism were to a large extent a result of the region's extreme aridity, which made agricultural and urban

---

[113] Irma Taddia, 'At the Origin of the State/Nation Dilemma: Ethiopia, Eritrea, Ogaden in 1941', *Northeast African Studies*, 12(2–3), 1990, 157–170.

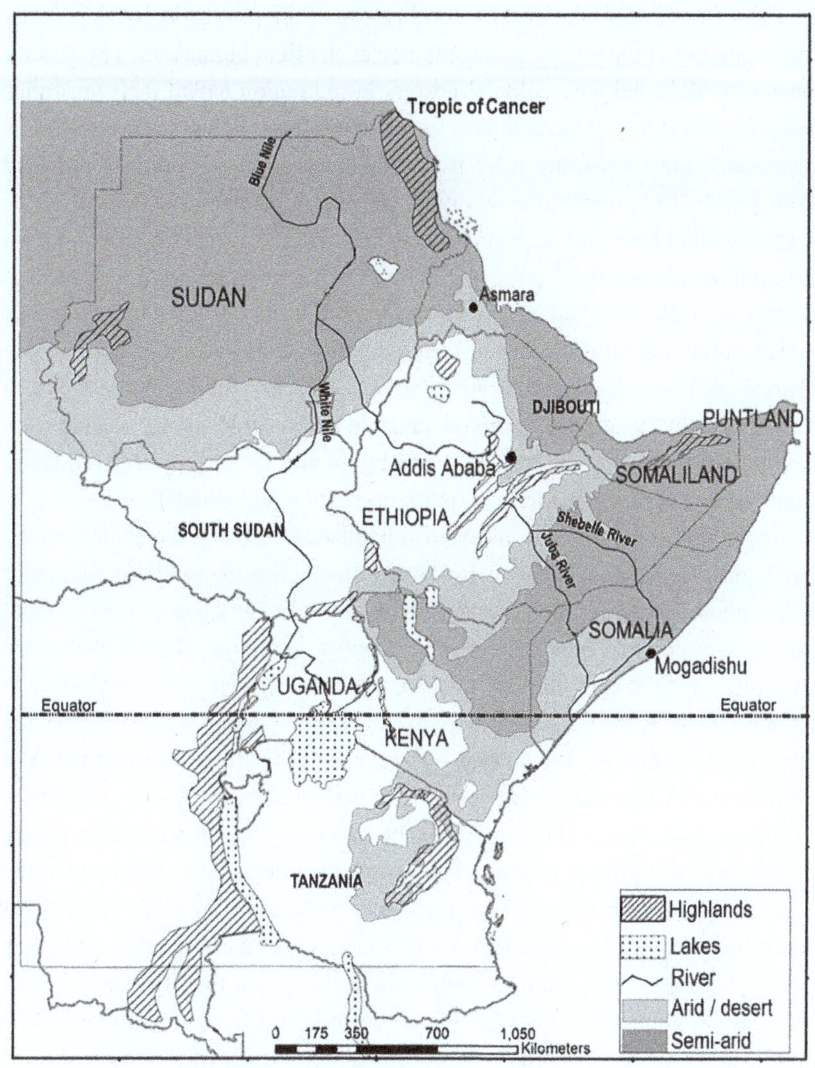

Map 3 Northeast Africa, present.

Source: Author, based on data in the public domain.

development difficult. One constant factor was the failure of states to grow big enough to control large territories, affecting precolonial and colonial states alike.

Most of the historiography concerns the absence of state-like institutions almost anywhere before European colonization.[114] Instead, the 'political

---

[114] See discussion on the subject in David D. Laitin and Said S. Samatar, *Somalia: Nation in Search of a State*, Boulder, CO: Westview Press, 1987.

structure … reflected the decentralised nature of the production base'.[115] The fragmentation of the power base continued even after colonialism. This feature helps to understand why colonial powers in the region called their territories protectorates rather than colonies: a protectorate is a declaration to act as a caretaker until a worthy ruler is found. In contrast, a colony is obtained from a ruler. The protectorate was more common in the Horn of Africa.

On the other hand, the seaboard was an active trading zone for millennia. On the northern side of the Horn of Africa, the major ports before the nineteenth century were Berbera and Zeila (Saylac) in present-day Somaliland, Suakin in Sudan, about 600 miles north and facing the Red Sea, Massawa in present-day Eritrea, located roughly between these two extreme points, and Mocha in Yemen. The African ports received valuable cargo (gold, ivory, slaves) from the interior and exported these by sea to Egypt and West Asia. Gujarati cloth, sugar, iron, and rice came to these ports from Surat and Bombay.

Mocha traded coffee from the Yemen highlands. In the seventeenth century, the English East India Company discovered Mocha was the principal market for Indian goods bound for the Levant. They tried to capture a part of the trade, but that attempt angered the Surat merchants and their patron, the Mughal court. Gujaratis stayed in control of the trade between the northern ports and India. On the southern side, the Benadir coast, Mogadishu was a major seaport. Unlike the other ports in this list, Mogadishu was near an agricultural area that received irrigation water from two river basins. In the early nineteenth century, cultivation of millets grew in parts of this combined basin, increasing the demand for slaves.

The caravan traffic did not go very far into the interior. The other end of the caravan traffic with the northern ports was Sennar on the Blue Nile, about 400 miles west of Massawa, Kassala in Sudan, located even closer, and a few market towns in the Ethiopian highlands. In between, there was a desert to cross. Road connection between the coast and the Ethiopian highlands was poor. Massawa was the link between the Ethiopian capital, Gondar, next to Lake Tana, the source of the Blue Nile, and the coast. It was a difficult journey; still, Massawa was rather more integrated with the interior than the other ports.

With an interest in the Red Sea trade in spices, the Ottoman Empire sponsored and governed the northern ports from the sixteenth until the nineteenth century, but with a light touch, via a governor who resided in Suakin and had few resources, military or bureaucratic. Local power resided with the chiefs. The Ottoman interest was in protecting sea trade and, even more, hajj pilgrim traffic.

---

[115] Abdi Samatar, 'The State, Agrarian Change and Crisis of Hegemony in Somalia', *Review of African Political Economy*, 43, 1988, 26–41. Cited text on p. 29.

The interior did not interest them. These ports also developed close ties with Yemen thanks to linguistic, political, and commercial links. The Sultanate of Yemen became a British protectorate in 1886. Aden, which the British had acquired exactly fifty years before, had emerged as an economic centre in the Red Sea. Aden reinforced both Yemeni and British interests in the Northeast African coast. In the south, the Zanzibar Sultanate claimed the Benadir coastland but had little solid presence there. Power was held by local chiefs ruling over smaller areas. Beyond the ports, a vast pastoralist hinterland made building stable fiscal states a complex enterprise.

In effect, political power and religious affiliations were deeply fragmented. Historians have often called the pastoralist environments 'societies where states do not fit well' or 'economies without states'.[116] Terms like these appear frequently in descriptions of Somalia. The sultanates to the south in the river basins resembled states. Elsewhere, states were hardly more solid than a network of clans. While every state or clan attempted to profit from trade, raids on wrecked European ships in the hazardous stretch of the Indian Ocean close to the Ras Haafuun (or Xaafuun) cape were a more profitable activity. When big pan-regional conflicts broke out, such as the Mahdist wars of 1881–99 between Anglo-Egyptian rule and the Sudanese Mahdiyya, these clans (and sometimes the seaports) fought each other. Throughout the nineteenth century, sectarian strife was widespread.

Why was the Horn an ungovernable space? The answer is that states had no secure tax base. Animal herding was the main occupation in the interior, and mobile herders were notoriously tricky to tax because they did not own a fixed and well-defined asset (pastures and animal stock rose and fell). Agricultural land occupied a very small part of the land area. Trade earned sound money, but not nearly enough. This complex of features, which kept local states too small and fragmented, also kept in check the imperialist ambitions of the major powers in the area, whether Ottoman, Ismail Pasha of Egypt in the 1860s, Ethiopia, and earlier, the sixteenth-century warlord Ahmed Gran. Several agents wanted to govern the coastlands but found the military enterprise and the governance beyond their capacity. I will argue later that the same features also constrained the imperialism of the British, French, and Italian varieties. At the same time, because no hegemonic power emerged in northeast Africa, trade remained relatively free from the control of big states.

The conflicts might have made European colonization an easy affair. However, the drive to colonize was not strong on behalf of the British and the French. Besides the difficulty of creating a fiscally viable state, the economic interest

---

[116] William Reno, review of Peter D. Little, *Somalia: Economy without State*, Bloomington, IN: Indiana University Press, 2003, in *Journal of Modern African Studies*, 42(3), 2004, 474–475.

needed to be more vital for all Europeans. Until the mid nineteenth century, the coastlands and seaports on the Gulf of Aden and the Red Sea held little economic interest for Britain, serving merely as a stopover on a Mediterranean route to India. Britain's interest in the region was mainly political.

In 1799, Britain acquired a base in the region to prevent Napoleon from using Egypt to attack India. After the wars, Britain stayed on to ensure that no other European powers controlled the area. Increasingly, its foreign policy was based on two motivations: to stop the slave trade and ensure the indigenous states remained in control. While economics was secondary, a series of trade treaties signed between Ethiopia and Somali chiefs and warlords, on the one hand, and France and Britain, on the other, did reduce trade barriers and kept checks on colonial rivalry. However, these were pre-emptive measures and did not lead to a commercial expansion.

With the British occupation of Aden, a trade network emerged in the Red Sea area, with bases in Gujarat and Bombay. Access to trade benefited from community control on credit and shipping. This was not the first time Western India and the Horn were connected. A much older traffic of people and soldiers had already created Afro-Indian communities on the Indian side. However, commercial links strengthened since the nineteenth century, indirectly via the expansion of British power.

Some early nineteenth-century reports said Massawa was home to Gujarati Hindu merchants with a near monopoly of specific trades.[117] The Indians were nervous that the Suez Canal would hurt their trade. Twenty years later, Italian colonization was another worry for the Indians. On balance, however, the opening of the Canal marked a positive change. It ensured the safe passage of ships to and from India, greatly encouraging trade both towards Europe and towards India and solidifying the moderate British presence in the area.

Because of the treaties and the start of the Canal in 1869, commerce started to grow in these ports from the end of the nineteenth century. Although I have yet to see any data to suggest how much it grew, statements like the following do occur frequently. 'In the second half of the 19th century', write two modern scholars of the history of these ports, 'Red Sea trade jumped up suddenly after the gradual decline for nearly two centuries'.[118] Jonathan Miran's study of Massawa confirms this trend and broad-based commercialization.[119]

---

[117] Richard Pankhurst, 'The "Banyan" or Indian Presence at Massawa, the Dahlak Islands and the Horn of Africa', *Journal of Ethiopian Studies*, 12(1),1974, 185–212.

[118] Riichi Miyake and Rumi Okazaki, 'Study on the Trading Routes Connecting the Red Sea and Ethiopia as Serial Heritages', *Bulletin of the Fuji Women's University*, 49, Ser. II, 2012, 23–38. Cited text on p. 32.

[119] Jonathan Miran, 'Facing the Land, Facing the Sea: Commercial Transformation and Urban Dynamics in the Red Sea Port of Massawa, 1840s-1900s', PhD Dissertation of University of Michigan, 2004.

There was, in fact, considerable churning in the trade, which led to a concentration of trading in fewer places than before. Slave trading persisted in this area for almost a century after its abolition by the British. As late as 1892, the London illustrated weekly *The Graphic* printed a picture of the slave market in Khartoum, a busy place filled with merchants on horseback. Along the coast, Zanzibar was the primary slave market, Suakin was a close second. European expansion, directly and indirectly, led to a decline in the trade. Several sultanates and merchants in the region resisted that interference. Slaves worked mainly on farms in southern Somalia. Farming declined with the formal end of the trade from the 1870s, and agricultural lands returned to a bush state. Freed slaves left the region to go to Mombasa, among other towns. Coffee exports from Java and the rise of Aden damaged Mocha's trade in the nineteenth century. Much of the trade in Indian goods shifted to Aden. In the second half of the nineteenth century, trade shifted from Zeila and Suakin towards Massawa. Massawa was better suited as a deep-water port and was better for steamships. It was in a relatively well-watered if a very narrow (twenty-mile wide) stretch of the coast east of the highlands.

Although caravan trade may have declined, a compensating good emerged from the turn of the twentieth century to replace the lost business many times over – animals and hides. From India and Europe came guns, for which there was a flexible demand among the sultanates in Northeast Africa. The caravan traffic was not vital anymore. The animal trade started in arid pastoralist lands and was controlled by different merchants using different transport systems. The nineteenth century saw Massawa reach its height as a centre for trade. Cattle, hides, coffee, marine products, and cereals dominated the Red Sea trade. It was then home to a population that was both diverse and cosmopolitan. Pastoralists from Ethiopia came to work as labourers. Merchants came from India. Hadhrami (originating in the Hadhramaut region of southern Yemen) and Arab merchants and shippers were prominent, as they were in several East African ports.

Even if the scale of trade rose, the seaports had limited room for population growth and agglomeration. The ports had almost no agricultural land to sustain themselves and had to import food, sometimes water. The rivers in the region lost water in the dry months. Urban historians studying old settlements suggest the dependence of settlements on wells, which were few in the centre of the towns. One account explains Mocha's long-term decline: 'Mocha is on a sandy, arid stretch of the coast, and blowing sand and inadequate water supply have contributed to its decline.'[120] Mocha's water supply was largely imported from

---

[120] Kenneth Fletcher, 'Mocha', Encyclopedia Britannica, www.britannica.com/place/Mocha-Yemen.

a place twenty-four miles away. In the 1880s, a massive famine followed by epidemics broke out. The exact origins remain unknown. The Mahdist wars had affected trade and trade routes in the interior and pitted tribes against other tribes. In this geography, wars almost always involved cutting off food and water supplies to the rival peoples, a strategy relatively easy to follow because there were few targets to attack. By 1890, the population had halved in some areas due to these disasters.

Thus, the minimal resource base restricted the population the city could sustain and the prospects that commercialization would lead to a concentration of capital, finance, and skills and create cities that further strengthened state power. Access to the interior was always difficult and never significantly improved because railways did not develop. The deserts formed a barrier between the Somalian coastland and new colonies in the Rift Valley, and the Ethiopian highlands and swamps of South Sudan were barriers to accessing Egypt and Sudan from the coastland. The scarcity of European investment in the Horn of Africa and the prevalence of pastoralism weakened the drive to build communication. The only railway in the region was a French construction that connected Djibouti with Addis Ababa. Despite carrying coffee, leather, and some illegal arms, it was not a commercially significant line.

For all these reasons, the colonization process was half-hearted rather than a planned conquest. Geography was the key to explaining why. '[T]he most simple explanation for imperialism, the straightforward desire for land', wrote the historian David Hamilton, 'has ... been a ... factor – but with a distinctive variation. So harsh and unattractive is the Somali hinterland that the various imperial Powers, perhaps from the Sabeans of old and certainly from the Turks in the sixteenth century to the British in the nineteenth, have regularly been satisfied by merely keeping possible rivals out'.[121]

At the end of the nineteenth century, with the expansion of the army in India, the British anxiety that the Red Sea had some role in the defence and prosperity of India had been significantly reduced. Economics was never a paramount concern for the Europeans who came to this coastland. Dealing with Ethiopia, the most significant state, mattered more to the British. Against that backdrop, when Italian interest in the northern Horn of Africa grew, the British did not resist. The Italians had already established themselves on the Benadir coast by browbeating the Zanzibar Sultan and received Eritrea from Menelik, a contender for the Ethiopian throne. Italian interest, again, was not primarily economic but political: to capture Ethiopia. This ambition received a massive

---

[121] David Hamilton, 'Imperialism Ancient and Modern: A Study of British Attitudes to the Claims to Sovereignty to the Northern Somali Coastline', *Journal of Ethiopian Studies*, 5(2), 1967, 9–35. Cited text on p. 33.

setback in 1896 as the best effort to conquer Ethiopia had to be given up. It was given up not only because of resistance but also because the invading army found it impossible to survive in the arid and desert areas in the northeast of Ethiopia.

Despite the meat and animal trade through Benadir, the Horn of Africa lost significance as a trading zone to Aden in the north and Mombasa in the south in the early twentieth century. Italian colonization tried to make its territories economically sensible acquisitions but failed. Miran shows that this 'small, barren, unbearably hot and dry' acquisition disillusioned the Italians about its worth.[122] Massawa had a small and largely barren hinterland from which to draw goods. Extreme aridity and seasonality regulated caravan trade. The port was too resource-constrained to expand much. A policy to promote settler farmers failed because of scarcity of water.

Thus frustrated, Italian colonization shifted the primary economic hub towards the new capital, Asmara, which was on the cooler highlands. Considerable investment went into construction until the interwar period. But Asmara evolved more as a military base than as a commercial hub. Massawa's best years were coming to an end. In the early twentieth century, Asmara and other regional hubs took the stage, and the town's downfall was exacerbated by Eritrea's protracted war for independence in the years that followed.

From 1900, if not earlier, the axis of long-distance trade shifted from the Horn of Africa towards Aden and Mombasa. Of these two ports, Aden had no hinterland to speak of, but it was a transit port, a coaling station, and a naval base, so closely integrated with India that the British Empire was concerned to keep it going, whether or not it made economic sense. Almost right across the sea, 120 miles to the west, in Obock (Djibouti), the French built their refuelling station. But 'its isolation, intense heat, and lack of vegetation' left Obock an insignificant port and a punishment post for French colonial officers.[123] What about Mombasa?

Trade, Colonialism, and Urban Spaces: East Africa

When the first European settlements appeared in East Africa in the late sixteenth century, the seaboard was ruled by city-states. These towns had trade ties to China, India, Arabia, and the Persian Gulf ports. These were located near the equator in a resource-rich landscape, with fertile river deltas and an extensive fishing industry. It does not seem, however, that the hinterland mattered for tax purposes. The entire energy of the city-states had been focused on capturing maritime trade. The city's elite lived on the profits of trade. In turn, they invested

---

122 Miran, 'Facing the Land, Facing the Sea'. P. 25

123 Charles J. Balesi, 'Henry de Monfreid: Chronicler and Adventurer of the Red Sea', *Proceedings of the Meeting of the French Colonial Historical Society*, 5, 1980, 83–87. Cited text on p. 83.

in building strong defences and connected with other seaboard areas, like Sofala to the south, which was the endpoint of gold traffic.

They were also endpoints of caravan trade, bringing traded goods and slaves from the interior. The caravan trade followed several routes, the most important ones connecting the Lake region with seaboard towns, principally Zanzibar and Kilwa. Another significant point about their geography is that 'most settlements were located on islands slightly off the mainland to guard against mainland tribe incursions'.[124] The inland situation also offered ships safer anchorage.

These states fought often. The conflicts between the city-states and within the ruling families were why some declined, and some survived before British and German colonization of the coast in the late nineteenth century. The Portuguese garrisoned Kilwa in the early sixteenth century, but the town was already in decline, its dependency on Sofala having broken away.

Zanzibar, by contrast, flourished. Again, an island port, Zanzibar was 'sufficiently distant from the mainland to be safe from invasions by a tribe which is not already sea-faring'.[125] Still, Zanzibar's strength did not derive from the sea alone. Set up by settlers from the Middle East, its benign climate and plentiful monsoon rains made the soil highly fertile. The locals could grow a variety of crops for their use. Later, the Portuguese found the place to be a convenient source of food grains, more precisely, supplies of provisions to Portuguese ships.

The Portuguese interest in capturing some of the most profitable trades in the region, especially gold, weakened the city-states in the East African seaboard. How much trade changed hands is unclear. The elites fought harder to keep control.[126] Zanzibar's rule changed several times from the early sixteenth century until the early eighteenth century, but its economic base was sound enough to survive the turmoil. The port government continued as before; only the governor had to report to different masters.

From the second or third decade of the eighteenth century, Zanzibar started exporting slaves to Muscat, India, Mauritius, and the Persian Gulf. In the nineteenth century, the slave trade rose considerably, but it was not the primary source of the town's profit. The Omani rulers succeeded in maintaining Zanzibar's role as an entrepot, and one of them (Sayyid Said) even contemplated developing local agriculture for future settlements by immigrants from arid Oman, though not much happened on that front.

---

[124] John Spencer Trimingham, cited in Terry H. Elkiss, 'Kilwa Kisiwani: The Rise of an East African City-State', *African Studies Review*, 16(1), 1973, 119–130.

[125] Jan Knappert, 'A Short History of Zanzibar', *Annales Aequatoria*, 13, 1992, 15–37. Cited text on p. 18.

[126] Knappert, 'A Short History of Zanzibar'.

Before the colonization of East Africa in the last decade of the nineteenth century, British interest in the region had taken two forms. One of them was a multinational enterprise engaged in suppressing the slave trade. The Zanzibar slave market was a significant focus of that mission. Second, the India-Muscat-Aden-Africa trade was by then well established. East African colonization was, in a way, an extension of British power already entrenched in India, just as the colonization encouraged an extension of Indian overseas capitalism. The Indian traders and bankers settled in Muscat as financiers and tax collectors before Zanzibar became a British protectorate (1890). The commercial and economic links became more direct after the political shift. Indian firms operated the Zanzibar customs for some time.[127]

East African colonization followed a third dynamic – besides anti-slavery moves and building maritime trade links with India. This third process involved integrating the economies of the seaboard and the interior, especially the resource-rich Lake region of Africa. Following the Berlin Conference (1885) and several treaties with the local rulers, Britain began to colonize the Kenyan coast in 1885. Progress into the interior was erratic and happened through conflicts and alliances. In 1888, after an agreement between the shipping magnate William Mackinnon and the British Foreign Office, the Imperial British East Africa Company (IBEA) was established. Mackinnon and his associates were to fund the subsequent explorations and negotiate treaties, in which the earlier treaties negotiated by Henry Johnston, explorer, naturalist, and political mediator, were useful.

The company's interest was in trade in ivory, among other goods. Suppressing the slave trade from Zanzibar by intervening in the source of the trade was also a stated objective. Undoubtedly, many individuals engaged in extending British and German power in East Africa believed in that aim. But it was mixed up with other aims. The Company failed in 1894. But its work was done. In 1895, the British formally took over Kenya (East Africa Protectorate) and Uganda.[128]

A similar set of processes were at work in Mombasa, where these delivered more dramatic results. Mombasa is a coralline island situated sufficiently inland to have a sheltered position, with deep water on both sides for ships to come in. It has been a trading centre on the Swahili Coast for centuries. The town was connected to the interior by overland routes. However, until the railways in the late nineteenth century, Mombasa's significance derived mainly from its connections with other ports in East Africa and other Indian Ocean territories, including India and the Arabian Peninsula. Local rulers were practically

[127] Padma Srinivasan, 'Indian Traders in Zanzibar with Special Reference to Jairam Shewji (19th Century)', *Proceedings of the Indian History Congress*, 61, 2000–2001, 1142–1148.

[128] Jonas Fossli Gjersø, 'The Scramble for East Africa: British Motives Reconsidered, 1884–95', *Journal of Imperial and Commonwealth History*, 43(5), 2015, 831–860.

autonomous. In the eighteenth century, the Mazrui dynasty ruled the city as representatives of the Imams of Oman. The city then became a part of the Zanzibar Sultanate before it became a British Protectorate in 1895.[129]

Histories of Mombasa suggest that despite these advantages, the old trading order protected by the Swahili elite and represented by the old port declined after British colonization. However, Mombasa's economy received a new life with rail and road communication connecting the port with Uganda. Even before formal colonization, the IBEA had initiated such a project. The Uganda railway began while the IBEA was still in charge. In the early twentieth century, Mombasa's 'rise to predominance as the chief commercial center of East Africa' had owed much to the railway. The railway reduced transport costs, made human porterage obsolete, brought new areas within the commercial orbit of the city, and 'facilitated a phenomenal increase in the size of the commercial community' in all East Africa.[130] A significant part of that flow of capital and labour originated in British India.

Conclusion

The key takeaway from the section is that coastland had a natural and significant advantage in a semi-arid tropical environment – the premise of the whole Element – but when aridity was pervasive and extreme, coastal cities had limited chance to forge connections inland and grow by drawing in capital and skills. In that condition, European colonial rule originated in political designs and anxieties, focused mainly on politics, and had a limited connection with the region's economy.

If the origin of modern imperialism seems too abstract a reason to read the narrative offered in this Element, there can be another, more direct route to the topic: cities. Some of the world's largest cities originated in intercontinental trade by the sea *in colonial times*, roughly the nineteenth and early twentieth centuries (Bombay, Calcutta, Madras, Jakarta, Lagos, Mombasa, Abidjan, … the list goes on). The wealthy elite of the cities implicitly or otherwise backed European rule, securing it. What was the connection between places and power and between urbanism and colonialism? European merchants operated from numerous sites on the seaboard. Not all grew or became military-political centres, but some did. The Element explores what conditions made them succeed in this way.

In the arid tropics, a place's chances of growing depended on food and water security in the presence of a pervasive threat of droughts and famines.

---

[129] Rosemary McConkey and Thomas McErlean, 'Mombasa Island: A Maritime Perspective'. *International Journal of Historical Archaeology*, 11(2), 2007, 99–121; Fred James Berg, 'The Swahili Community of Mombasa, 1500–1900', *Journal of African History*, 9(1), 1968, 35–56.

[130] Karim Kassam Janmohammed, 'A History of Mombasa, c. 1895–1939: Some Aspects of Economic and Social Life in an East African Port Town during Colonial Rule', PhD Dissertaton of Northwestern University, 1978, 44–45.

Commercial prospects also depended on access to the interior and what the interior could offer for trade. If these conditions were present, some places could grow by drawing indigenous capital and concentrating wealth and power while weakening the rival cities in the interior. That capitalism, operating from sites of intercontinental trade, reinforced colonialism. If the conditions were absent, places might continue as trading hubs but not much more.

The earlier sections showed how that concentration happened in India. I have now shown that it was present in Northeast Africa but was significantly weaker as a force than in South Asia. Massawa saw population growth, and yet, at its height in 1900, it had one-tenth the population of Bombay, and the two were growing further apart. The seaside had a significant climate advantage when the interior was arid or semi-arid. However, any state's drive and capacity to integrate the inland and coastland would be weak if the former was too arid and unpromising commercially. This was Northeast Africa, where colonial power ruled from a distance.

Elsewhere, the concentration process and integration of the seaboard and the interior happened differently. Several major colonial port cities were transit ports, like Batavia, interconnecting island economies rather than the seaboard with terrestrial space. Some, like Lagos or Mombasa, were equatorial and not particularly resource-scarce. In all cases where a powerful direct rule emerged, the colonial powers staked money and energy to advance spatial integration, with much help from indigenous capitalists. Colonial railways and politics supplanted caravan and slave trades but worked to strengthen the integration, sometimes to promote trade and sometimes to link up isolated colonial domains. When the integration took off, agglomeration happened.

Postscript

I realize that the text offered must read like a proposal for an interpretation of the origin of modern imperialism rather than a fully substantiated thesis. However, my purpose is served if this proposal (1) induces empire historians to take the environment seriously and (2) aids the search for a pattern underlying the diverse ways colonialism emerged in the nineteenth-century world.

Appendix: Change of Place Names

Old name in sources	Present-day official name/alternatives
Baliapatam	Valapattanam
Bombay	Mumbai
Calcutta	Kolkata
Madras	Chennai
Broach	Bharuch
Mysore	Mysuru
Tumkur	Tumakuru
Tellicherry	Thalassery
Cochin	Kochi
Kerala	Keralam
Palghat	Palakkad
Calicut	Kozhikode
Cannanore	Kannur
Orissa	Odisha
Vizagapatam	Visakhapatnam
Petapole	Peddapalli
Pondicherry	Puducherry
Benares	Banaras, Varanasi
Bantam	Banten
Massawa	Mitsiwa
Mogadiscio	Mogadishu
Zeila	Saylac
Benadir	Banaadir
Macassar	Makassar
Celebes	Sulawesi

Bibliography

Anon., *Reflections on the Present Commotion in Bengal*, London: J. Kearsly, 1764.

Anon., *An Historical Account of the Settlement and Possession of Bombay by the East India Company*, London: W. Richardson, 1781.

Anon., 'Journal of a Residence in Great Britain, by Jehungeer Nowrajee and Hirjeebhoy Merwanjee, of Bombay, Naval Architects. London. 1841', *Calcutta Review*, 4, 1845, Miscellaneous Notices, i–xii.

Arasaratnam, Sinnapah, 'The Politics of Commerce in the Coastal Kingdoms of Tamil Nad 1650–1700', *South Asia: Journal of South Asian Studies*, 1(1), 1971, 1–19.

Arasaratnam, Sinnapah, 'Factors in the Rise, Growth and Decline of Coromandel Ports CIRCA 1650–1720', *South Asia: Journal of South Asian Studies*, 7(2), 1984, 19–30.

Balesi, Charles J., 'Henry de Monfreid: Chronicler and Adventurer of the Red Sea', *Proceedings of the Meeting of the French Colonial Historical Society*, 5, 1980, 83–87.

Barua, Pradep P., 'Maritime Trade, Seapower, and the Anglo-Mysore Wars, 1767–1799', *The Historian*, 73(1), 2011, 22–40.

Basu, Susan Neild, 'Madras in 1800: Perceiving the City', *Studies in the History of Art*, 31, 1993, 221–240

Bayly, Christopher Alan, *Rulers, Townsmen and Bazaars: North India Society in the Age of British Expansion 1770–1870*, Cambridge: Cambridge University Press, 1983, 5.

Berg, Fred James, 'The Swahili Community of Mombasa, 1500–1900', *Journal of African History*, 9(1), 1968, 35–56.

Bernier, François, *Travels in the Mogul Empire AD 1656–1668*, London: Humphrey Milford, 1916.

Bhattacharyya, Debjani, *Empire and Ecology in the Bengal Delta: The Making of Calcutta*, New York: Cambridge University Press, 2018.

Biddulph, John *Stringer Lawrence: The Father of the Indian Army*, London: John Murray, 1901.

Boxer, Charles Ralph 'The Dutch Economic Decline', in Carlo M. Cipolla, ed., *The Economic Decline of Empires*, Abingdon: Routledge, 2006, 235–263.

Broeze, Frank, ed., *Brides of the Sea, Port Cities of Asia from the 16th-20th Centuries*, Kensington: New South Wales University Press, 1989.

Buchanan, Francis, *A Journey from Madras through The Countries of Mysore, Canara, and Malabar*, London: T. Cadell, and W. Davies, 1807.

Das Gupta, Ashin, 'Indian Merchants and the Western Indian Ocean: The Early Seventeenth Century', *Modern Asian Studies*, 19(3), 1985, 481–499.

Dasgupta, Ashin, 'The Maritime Merchant and Indian History', *South Asia: Journal of South Asian Studies*, 7(1), 1984, 27–33.

Early American Studies (special issue), 15(4), 2017, 649–659.

Elkiss, Terry H., 'Kilwa Kisiwani: The Rise of an East African City-State', *African Studies Review*, 16(1), 1973, 119–130.

Fawcett, Charles, *The English Factories in India, vol. 4 (New Series) The Eastern Coast and Bay of Bengal 1670–1677*, Oxford: Clarendon Press, 1955.

Fletcher, Kenneth, 'Mocha', Encyclopedia Britannica, www.britannica.com/place/Mocha-Yemen, 2024.

Foster, William, *The English Factories in India 1630–33*, Oxford: Clarendon Press, 1910.

Foster, William, *The English Factories in India 1634–36*, Oxford: Clarendon Press, 1911.

Foster, William, *The English Factories in India 1646–50*, Oxford: Clarendon Press, 1914.

Foster, William, *The English Factories in India 1655–60*, Oxford: Clarendon Press, 1921.

Foster, William, *The English Factories in India 1661–64*, Oxford: Clarendon Press, 1923.

Foster, William, *The English Factories in India 1668–1669*, Oxford: Clarendon Press, 1927.

Gani, Shahabuddin M., 'Danish Settlement of Balasore', *Proceedings of the Indian History Congress*, 22, 1959, 354–357.

Gjersø, Jonas Fossli, 'The Scramble for East Africa: British Motives Reconsidered, 1884–95', *Journal of Imperial and Commonwealth History*, 43(5), 2015, 831–860.

Greville, Charles, *British India Analyzed The Provincial and Revenue Establishments of Tippoo Sultaun and of Mahomedan and British Conquerors in Hindoostan Stated and Considered*, London: E.Jefferey, J. Debrett and P. Elmsley, 1793.

Guha, Sumit, 'Rethinking the Economy of Mughal India: Lateral Perspectives', *Journal of the Economic and Social History of the Orient*, 58(4), 2015, 532–575.

Hamilton, David, 'Imperialism Ancient and Modern: A Study of British Attitudes to the Claims to Sovereignty to the Northern Somali Coastline', *Journal of Ethiopian Studies*, 5(2), 1967, 9–35.

Hasan, Farhat, 'Indigenous Cooperation and the Birth of a Colonial City: Calcutta, c. 1698–1750', *Modern Asian Studies*, 26(1), 1992, 65–82.

Hemingway, F. R., *Madras District Gazetteers. Trichinopoly,* Madras: Government Press, 1907.

Hoffman, Philip, *Why Did Europe Conquer the World?* Princeton: Princeton University Press, 2015.

Hopkins, A.G., 'Economic Imperialism in West Africa: Lagos, 1880–92', *Economic History Review*, 21(3), 1968, 580–606.

House of Lords, *Copies and Extracts of such Parts of the Correspondence between the Governor General, and the Governments of India respectively, with the Court of Directors, and the Secret Committee thereof, as Relate to Hostilities with the Late Tippoo Sultan*, 1799, 63.

Jagtap, Neelambari, 'Ports, Markets, Commercial Networks, and Politics: Case of Tal (South) Konkan in the 17th Century', in Radhika Seshan and Ryuto Shimada, eds., *Connecting the Indian Ocean World: Across Sea and Land*, London: Routledge, 2022, 83–92.

Janmohammed, Karim Kassam, 'A History of Mombasa, c. 1895–1939: Some Aspects of Economic and Social Life in an East African Port Town during Colonial Rule', PhD Dissertaton of Northwestern University, 1978.

Karak, Anirban, 'The Politics of Commerce in Eighteenth-Century Bengal: A Reappraisal', *Indian Economic and Social History Review*, early-view 61(1), 2024, 33–66.

Karaman, K. Kivanç and Sevket Pamuk, 'Ottoman State Finances in European Perspective, 1500– 1914', *Journal of Economic History*, 70, 2010, 593–629 (along with www.ata.boun.edu.tr/sevketpamuk/ JEH2010articledatabase).

Khan, Mohibbul Hasan, *History of Tipu Sultan*, Calcutta and Dacca: The Bibliophile, 1951.

Knappert, Jan, 'A Short History of Zanzibar', *Annales Aequatoria*, 13, 1992, 15–37.

Kosambi, Damodar, *The Culture and Civilisation of Ancient India in Historical Outline*, London: Routledge and Kegan Paul, 1965.

Kroef, Justus M. van der, 'The Decline and Fall of the Dutch East India Company', *The Historian*, 10(2), 1948, 118–134.

Laitin, David D. and Said S. Samatar, *Somalia: Nation in Search of a State*, Boulder: Westview Press, 1987.

Lee, Robert, 'The Socio-economic and Demographic Characteristics of Port Cities: A Typology for Comparative Analysis?' *Urban History*, 25(2), 1998, 147–72.

MacMunn, George Fletcher, *The Armies of India*, London: Adam and Charles Black, 1911.

Manucci, Niccolao, *Storia do Mogor*, 4 vols, London: John Murray, vol. 3, 390.

Marshall, Peter James, 'Presidential Address: Britain and the World in the Eighteenth Century: III, Britain and India', *Transactions of the Royal Historical Society*, 10, 2000, 1–16.

McConkey, Rosemary and Thomas McErlean, 'Mombasa Island: A Maritime Perspective', *International Journal of Historical Archaeology*, 11(2), 2007, 99–121.

Berg, Fred James, 'The Swahili Community of Mombasa, 1500–1900', *Journal of African History*, 9(1), 1968, 35–56.

Miran, Jonathan, 'Facing the Land, Facing the Sea: Commercial Transformation and Urban Dynamics in the Red Sea Port of Massawa, 1840s-1900s', PhD Dissertation of University of Michigan, 2004.

Mishra, Patit Paban, 'Balasore Port-Town in Seventeenth Century', *Proceedings of the Indian History Congress*, 59, 1998, 301–10.

Miyake, Riichi and Rumi Okazaki, 'Study on the Trading Routes Connecting the Red Sea and Ethiopia as Serial Heritages', *Bulletin of the Fuji Women's University*, 49, Ser. II, 2012, 23–38.

Moreland, William, *India at the Death of Akbar: An Economic Study*, London: Macmillan, 1920.

Mukherji, Bimala Prasad, 'The English Factory at Hooghly (1651–1690)', *Proceedings of the Indian History Congress*, 19, 1956, 290–300.

Nadri, Ghulam A., 'Exploring the Gulf of Kachh: Regional Economy and Trade in the Eighteenth Century', *Journal of the Economic and Social History of the Orient*, 51(3), 2008, 460–486.

Nadri, Ghulam A., *Eighteenth-Century Gujarat: The Dynamics of its Political Economy, 1750–1800*, Leiden: Brill, 2009.

Oak, Mandar and Anand Swamy, 'Myopia or Strategic Behavior? Indian Regimes and the East India Company in Late Eighteenth Century India', *Explorations in Economic History*, 49(3), 2012, 352–366.

O'Brien, Patrick, 'State Formation and Economic Growth: The Case of Britain, 1688–1846', in Jürgen Backhaus, ed., *Navies and State Formation: The Schumpeter Hypothesis Revisited and Reflected*, Berlin: LIT Verlag, 2012, 217–272.

Pankhurst, Richard, 'The "Banyan" or Indian Presence at Massawa, the Dahlak Islands and the Horn of Africa', *Journal of Ethiopian Studies*, 12(1),1974, 185–212.

Pearson, Michael, 'Littoral Society: The Concept and the Problems', *Journal of World History*, 17(4), 2006, 353–373.

Ray, Aniruddha, 'The Crisis of the French East India Company at Surat and Bengal at the End of the 17th Century', *Proceedings of the Indian History Congress*, 54, 1993, 361.

Ray, Aniruddha, 'Shorosh shatabdir sheshbhage Banglar nagarbinyas o artha-noitik samriddhi', [Urban and Economic Expansion in Bengal towards the End of the Sixteenth Century, in Bengali] in Gautam Chattopadhyay, ed., itihas Onusandhan [History Research], Calcutta: K.P. Bagchi, 1986, 20–34.

Reno, William, Review of Peter D. Little, *Somalia: Economy without State*, Bloomington, IN: Indiana University Press, 2003.

Roney, Jessica, 'Introduction: Distinguishing Port Cities, 1500–1800', *Early American Studies*, 15(4), 2017, 649–659.

Roy, Tirthankar, 'Rethinking the Origins of British India: State Formation and Military-fiscal Undertakings in an Eighteenth Century World Region', *Modern Asian Studies*, 47(4), 2013, 1125–1156.

Roy, Tirthankar, 'The Mutiny and the Merchants', *Historical Journal*, 59(2), 2016, 393–416.

Roy, Tirthankar, *An Economic History of India 1707–1857*, London: Routledge, 2021.

Roy, Tirthankar, *Monsoon Economies: India's History in a Changing Climate*, Cambridge MA: MIT Press, 2022.

Salimullah, *Tarikh I Bangal*, volume 2 of 2, trans. Francis Gladwin, Calcutta: J. W. Fischer of Stuart and Cooper, 1785,

Samatar, Abdi, 'The State, Agrarian Change and Crisis of Hegemony in Somalia', *Review of African Political Economy*, 43, 1988, 26–41.

Sarkar, Jagadish Narayan, 'Notes on Balasore and the English in the First Half of the Seventeenth Century', *Proceedings of the Indian History Congress*, 13, 1950, 209–21.

Seid-Gholam-Hossein-Khan, *Seir Mutaqherin*, vol. 3 of 3, Calcutta: T.D. Chatterjee, 1902, 388.

Sengupta, Kaustubh Mani, 'Bazaars, Landlords, and the Company Government in Late Eighteenth-Century Calcutta', *IESHR*, 52 (2), 2015, 121–146.

Seshan, Radhika, 'Coastal Connections of Fort St. George (Madras/Chennai) in the 17th Century', *Proceedings of the Indian History Congress*, 78, 2017, 372–379.

Shastri, Haraprasad, 'Baneshwar Bidyalankar', *Sahitya-Parishat-Patrika* [Bengali] 38, 1938, 135–144.

Shil, Shibchandra, Gaure Suarnabanik [Bengali, Subarnabaniks in Gaur], Chunchura: Author, 1910, 49.

Shimada, Ryuto, 'Southeast Asia and International Trade: Continuity and Change in Historical Perspective', in Keijiro Otsuka and Kaoru Sugihara, eds., *Paths to the Emerging State in Asia and Africa*, Singapore: Springer, 2019, 35–72.

Shimada, Ryuto, 'The Long-Term Pattern of Maritime Trade in Java from the Late Eighteenth Century to the Mid-Nineteenth Century', *Southeast Asian Studies*, 2(3), 2013, 475–497.

Srinivasan, Padma, 'Indian Traders in Zanzibar with Special Reference to Jairam Shewji (19th Century)', *Proceedings of the Indian History Congress*, 61, 2000–2001, 1142–1148.

Stern, Philip, *The Company-State: Corporate Sovereignty and the Early Modern Foundations of the British Empire in India*, New York: Oxford University Press, 2011.

Subrahmanyam, Sanjay, 'The "Pulicat Enterprise": Luso-Dutch Conflict in South-Eastern India, 1610–1640', *South Asia: Journal of South Asian Studies*, 9(2), 1986, 17–36.

Subrahmanyam, Sanjay, *The Political Economy of Commerce: Southern India 1500–1650*, Cambridge: Cambridge University Press, 1990.

Subramanian, Lakshmi, *Indigenous Capital and Imperial Expansion: Bombay, Surat and the West Coast*, New Delhi: Oxford University Press, 1996.

Swai, Bonaventure, 'East India Company and Moplah Merchants of Tellicherry: 1694–1800', *Social Scientist*, 8(1), 1979, 58–70.

Taddia, Irma, 'At the Origin of the State/Nation Dilemma: Ethiopia, Eritrea, Ogaden in 1941', *Northeast African Studies*, 12(2–3), 1990, 157–170.

Temple, Richard, ed., *Diaries of Streynsham Master (1675–1680)*, 2 vols., London: John Murray, 1911.

Thomas, M. Arun, 'Merchants, Markets and Merchandise: Strategy of English East India Company Trade in Tellicherry 1725–1750', PhD Dissertation of the University of Calicut, 2015.

Thomas, M. Arun and Asokan Mundon, 'Robert Adams: the Real Founder of English East India Company's Supremacy in Malabar', *IOSR Journal of Humanities and Social Science*, 20(5), 2015, 19–26.

Varkey, Joy, 'The Significance of Mahe in Eighteenth-Century French India', *Proceedings of the Indian History Congress*, 58, 1997, 295–302.

Washbrook, David, 'Review of Sinnapah Arasaratnam and Aniruddha Ray, Masulipatnam and Cambay: A History of Two Port Towns 1500–1800', *Journal of the Economic and Social History of the Orient*, 39(4), 1996, 465–467.

Wellen, Kathryn, 'The Danish East India Company's War against the Mughal Empire, 1642–1698', *Journal of Early Modern History*, 19(4), 2015, 439–461.

John Joseph Wallis

University of Maryland

John Joseph Wallis is Professor of Economics at the University of Maryland. He is also Research Associate of NBER, CEPR, CAGE, and Snider Center. His research focuses on how patterns of economic institutions change over time and how economic institutions interact with political institutions in a way that make both sustainable over time.

About the Series

The Elements in Economic History series showcases cutting-edge research by leading scholars in the field. Designed to make new scholarship accessible to a broad public of researchers, students and general readers, the volumes highlight the most exciting and productive recent trends, methods, and research questions in economic history.

Printed by Integrated Books International,
United States of America